FROM THE DISSIDENT RIGHT II

Essays 2013

John Derbyshire

VDARE FOUNDATION

www.vdare.com

About the Cover

At the height of the fuss about my being dropped from *National Review*, the leftist website *Gawker.com* asked if they could interview me. I agreed, and the interview was published on their website on April 9th, 2012 (http://gawker.com/5900452/i-may-give-up-writing-and-work-as-a-butler-interview-with-john-derbyshire).

The interviewer was Maureen O'Connor, whom I must say I found quite fair and sensible, as leftists go. For reasons unknown to me they illustrated the interview with a picture pulled off my website. An ancient unsuspected cesspool had collapsed in my back yard a year or so before. The picture showed me standing in the hole looking up. I have no idea why *Gawker* chose that picture. Some reference to the idiom "When you're in a hole, stop digging," perhaps? But I'm not digging in the picture, and my supposed fault was not one of wrongheaded persistence. I really have no idea.

The leftist brain cannot be fathomed. (Though the hole could: it was eight feet deep.)

— John Derbyshire

TABLE OF CONTENTS

ARTICLES FROM OTHER SOURCES

RADIO DERB

AFTERWORD

INTRODUCTION

Messages in a Bottle from a Castaway Conservative

By James Kirkpatrick

The former head of the American Conservative Union, David Keene, once bragged about how "thoughtful conservatives" had excluded "castaways" who were seen as undesirable by the movement. Keene of course, attempted to use the American Conservative Movement as a tool for "pay for play," soliciting "donations" from corporations in exchange for lobbying influence. The "thoughtful conservatives" of the Beltway Right were in fact simply proof of Eric Hoffer's admonition that every great cause begins as a movement, becomes a business, and eventually degenerates into a racket.

A "castaway," as the late Sam Francis noted, is someone who flees a doomed ship. In this case, Conservatism Inc. was the sinking ship and the castaways were the dissident conservatives floating away to safety. To expand the metaphor—this time the rats are *staying* on the ship—and the castaways are the men of integrity seeking out new shores.

Among the most distinguished of this hardy company is John Derbyshire. Like few others in a decadent time, John Derbyshire is a "competent man," as defined by Robert Heinlein. He has appeared in movies with Bruce Lee, worked with his hands, raised a beautiful family with his lovely wife Rosie, written books on mathematics and works of fiction, and remained a learnéd and entertaining commentator on a range of subjects that goes far beyond politics. All this while beating cancer. This is a man with a real life and something to say.

It's a measure of how far we have fallen that John Derbyshire was introduced to the mass public simply as a "racist," because of a column he wrote for *Takimag* on race relations. It led to one of those racial moral panics that historians of the future will marvel at just as we furrow our brows over the Nika riots or the Dutch tulip craze. He lost his position as a contributor at *National Review* but their loss was the Dissident Right's gain, as this freed him to bless *VDare* and other publications with his wit, humor and erudition on a consistent basis.

Most importantly, again like few of his contemporaries, he is a gentleman who handles difficulties with charm and poise. Even after being publicly attacked by former colleagues, he has always spoken well of his friends in the movement, exemplifying the kind of self-possession, confidence, and even irony that is all too often missing on the American Right.

As a fellow contributor to *VDare*, I confess a sense of envy as week after week, month after month, John Derbyshire dominates the "hits" on our website. It beggars belief that one man can contribute so much quality material on such a consistent basis. In a better time, he would be as well-known as a Samuel Johnson. But as even Johnson isn't widely recognized in the Age of Affirmative Action, the best we can do is offer this modest collection of his best work from 2013. The Revolution may not be right around the corner—but with ready access to John Derbyshire's observations on the passing scene, one can't help but think that the present isn't so bad after all.

SPEECHES

John Derbyshire's Address to the First *VDare* Webinar

January 24, 2013

[This is adapted from an address by John Derbyshire to the First *VDARE.com* Webinar on January 19, 2013. We hope to make recordings available shortly. For information when available, email office@vdare.com with "Webinar recording" in subject line.]

Introduction: Name, Rank, Serial Number

Good morning, ladies and gentlemen. My name is John Derbyshire. I am a freelance writer.

When I tell people that, quite a common response is: Yes, but what do you do for a *living?* Incredible to report, this *is* my living, and has been for the past twelve years. I have published four books and a CD, and self-published a fifth book. I have written a vast amount of fugitive journalism of the lower sort—opinionating, book reviews, travel diaries—all of which can be found on my website, johnderbyshire.com.

I was briefly the subject of widespread attention—widespread, I mean, by the standards of the world of opinion journalism, which is not *very* widespread—last Spring, at the time of the Trayvon Martin business.

Black journalists were writing solemn two-hanky pieces about how they have to give their kids "The Talk," to make them aware how dangerous white people are to them. In fact, of course, blacks are far more dangerous to whites than whites are to blacks, by a factor of about five to one on the Department of Justice's published statistics.

I wrote up for *Taki's Magazine* the kind of "Talk" a nonblack parent might give to his child, to apprise him of the facts about race in America. The leftists raised a hue and cry, and one of my main outlets, *National Review*, jumped on the bandwagon and banished me from their pages and screens.

My other conservative outlets showed stiffer spines, and you can read my stuff regularly at *Taki's Magazine* and *VDARE.com*, and occasionally at *The American Spectator*, *Claremont Review of Books*, *Academic Questions*, and a scattering of other publications. You can also hear my weekly podcast, Radio Derb, now hosted by *Taki's Magazine*. My thanks to the various proprietors for not having joined in the Leftist lynch mob.

The National Question: What Is the Answer?

VDARE.com is a website dedicated to news, research, and opinions relating to the National Question.

What *is* the National Question? Well, if you want it phrased as an actual question, I can't improve on the title that the late Professor Samuel Huntington gave to his final book, published in 2004: *Who Are We? That* is the National Question.

If that's the question, what's the answer? Again it's hard to improve on Huntington. Here is what he said:

> The [American philosophical-Constitutional] Creed is unlikely to retain its salience if Americans abandon the Anglo-Protestant culture in which it has been rooted. A multicultural America will, in time, become a multi-creedal America, with groups with different cultures espousing distinctive political values and principles rooted in their particular cultures.

The National Question thus embraces issues of immigration, population, race, culture, language, religion, and national identity. Those are the topics you will most frequently encounter on *VDARE.com*.

That's not to say you won't encounter other topics. We *VDARE.com* contributors are a lively lot, with active and enquiring minds. You might find yourself looking at a movie review, a table of sport statistics, or a blog post on education, crime, opera, or Chinese onomastics.

We stay mostly on-topic, though, and the topic is the National Question, with a particular emphasis on patriotic immigration reform.

That makes us seriously unpopular with some important and powerful people and institutions. Why? Let me try to explain.

The Dissident Personality: On Being a Good Citizen

Please permit me to quote myself. This is from Chapter Seven of my book *We Are Doomed* (a title which, I should say, was *not* intended as an answer to Prof. Huntington). The chapter topic is human nature.

> The ordinary modes of human thinking are magical, religious, social, and personal. We want our wishes to come true; we want the universe to care about us; we want the approval of those around us; we want to get even with that s.o.b who insulted us at the last tribal council. For most people, wanting to know the cold truth about the world is way, way down the list.

For those of us who write about the National Question, it's the *social* aspect of human nature that keeps pushing itself to the front of our minds.

The reason is that we are citizens living in society, like the rest of you. We are mostly of a law-abiding, bourgeois temperament. As my colleague James Fulford likes to say: We brush our teeth. We do not relish the sound of breaking glass. Like Sir Thomas More in the play, we think none harm, we speak none harm, we do none harm.

Why, then, are we unpopular? Why are we actually regarded as *dangerous* by multitudes of our fellow citizens?

The reason is, that if you conduct careful empirical inquiry into National Question issues, you often come up with results that throw doubt on the idols of the tribe—on what Kipling called "the Gods of the market-place."

That, to right-thinking citizens, is a very shocking thing to do. Recall that Socrates was tried and sentenced to death for "failing to acknowledge the gods that the city acknowledges." If you fail to acknowledge the gods that the city acknowledges, you are not a good citizen.

There is no need for the gods, the idols of the tribe, to be actual deities. They can be abstract principles welded together into an ideology. The dissidents who plagued the rulers of the old U.S.S.R., and who still plague the rulers of Communist China today—people like Alexander Solzhenitsyn, Vladimir Bukovsky, Wei Jingsheng and Liu Xiaobo—have been brought to trial in officially atheist states for the same reason Socrates was brought to trial in Athens: They failed to acknowledge the gods that the city acknowledges.

I was surprised to find, when living in Communist China, that citizens—including sensible and well-educated citizens, including people who grumbled about the system they lived under—*did not like these dissidents*. In their minds, private grumbling did not make you a bad citizen; but making a fuss with your complaints in public did. It was seen as a selfish indulgence. "He should think of his family," people would say; or, "He'll weaken the country behaving like that."

It would be impertinent for me, living a comfortable life and so far in no danger of being shipped to a labor camp—let alone of having to drink hemlock—to claim identity with the great dissidents of history. I will unblushingly claim some similarities of personality, though.

In our lesser way, we are dissidents, and *VDARE.com* is a dissident website. We do not acknowledge the gods that the city acknowledges, the idols of the tribe. As Socrates described the accusations against him in the *Apology*: We speculate about the earth above, and search into the earth beneath, and make the worse appear the better cause. People *hate* that!

How a tribe gets to have the idols it has, is an interesting question. Suffice it to say here that it rarely has much to do with reason or empirical inquiry.

But what *are* these idols of the tribe, these gods of the city, whom we fail to acknowledge?

Cultural Marxism: Oppressors and Oppressed

Western civilization at the present time is in thrall to a set of ideas and attitudes loosely called "Cultural Marxism." I say "loosely" because the fit with classical Marxism is in some respects not a very good one.

I don't much like this term "Cultural Marxism"; not out of any tender regard for the feelings of the people we use it against, but because I think it insults *actual* Marxism.

For all the horrors it engendered, and for all that it was a radically false view of human affairs, classical Marxism had some intellectual body to it. It was nonsense, but it was interesting nonsense, and inspired serious people to acts of heroism. My father-in-law, whom I liked and respected, was a lifelong Marxist; and I knew some of the older generation of European Marxists, the Arthur Koestler generation, people who had spent their youth running from city to city in Europe with the Gestapo at their heels. They were wrong, but they were brave and admirable.

Cultural Marxism is also nonsense, but nothing like as interesting. It is really a shallow, infantile and narcissistic set of notions, a way for people to feel themselves important without having to think too much, risk anything, or accept too much responsibility. Cultural Marxists do not put their lives on the line, as Koestler and his comrades did. For the most part, they just strike poses.

The central concept of Cultural Marxism, which it *does* owe to classical Marxism, is that some group of people is oppressing some other group.

Marx saw the Western world of his own time as one in which owners of capital were oppressing the proletariat, the working classes. He expected that when the contradictions in this system, the class antagonisms, became sufficiently acute, there would be a revolutionary change to a new and more just order of society.

Those contradictions eventually did become acute: in 1914, when the great nations of Europe all went to war against each other. To the shock and bafflement of the Marxists, however, the proletariat of Europe, instead of staging a social revolution, marched obediently off to war under their bourgeois officers.

But Lenin's revolution in Russia saved appearances sufficiently that many Marxists were able to convince themselves that this was History working itself out as the Master had foretold—in spite of the fact that Lenin's Russia, and even less Stalin's, bore scant resemblance to the society of justice and equality Marx had envisioned.

Other Marxists could not forgive the proletariat for their dereliction of duty. They threw them, as we say nowadays, under the bus, and from the 1920s on began searching around for a *surrogate proletariat*—some group somewhere that was suffering nobly under oppression by some other group.

They duly found such a group. In fact they found several: Colonized peoples, American blacks, then later women and homosexuals. By now there is an entire menagerie of surrogate proletariats, whose boundaries can hardly be computed: fat people, schizophrenics, transsexuals, the disabled, and so on.

It's all hard to square with classical Marxism. Classical Marxism, for example, rested on a materialist conception of history, human nature shaped by economic forces. How did material circumstances make you a homosexual? And again, Marx actually thought European colonialism was a *progressive* force, lifting colonized peoples up from less-developed economies like the "Asiatic Mode of Production" and accelerating their advance towards capitalism and thence socialism.

The Frankfurt School of Marxists, in the middle decades of the last century, brought in Freudianism to help shore up the edifice, and expressions like "false consciousness" and "oppressive tolerance" came into vogue. As Freud fell out of fashion, though, even these scraps of intellectual clothing fell away. By the time of the New Left in the 1960s, leftist revolutionary ideology had degenerated into a Cowboys-and-Indians model of society in which selfish and ignorant white Christian men were stamping on the faces of blacks, aborigines, women, homosexuals, Muslims, and the rest.

Some weeks ago I reported on *VDARE.com* about a conversation I'd had with some friends from the former Yugoslavia, an old peasant society only recently opened to the world, where Cultural Marxism is being zealously proselytized by emissaries from the European Union and George Soros's manifold organizations. It was, though, a source of some distress to Cultural Marxists over there that they had no black people to add color and vibrancy to the ranks of the oppressed. Then they hit on a solution: the Gypsies! So now the Gypsies are the surrogate blacks of the Balkans, recipients of Affirmative Action, set-asides for government contracts, characters in sentimental fiction, and the rest: *surrogate* surrogate proletarians!

These are the idols of the tribe today, the gods of the city, organized under this key notion of society as oppressors and oppressed. Lenin expressed it very pithily in Russian as "Кто? Кого?"—Who's the nominative, who's the accusative? Who is doing what to whom?

The oppressed themselves have become idols of the tribe, with a kind of sacral status. Our fellow-dissident Larry Auster has said, for example, that American blacks are holy objects, and that to criticize them in any general way is a kind of sacrilege. After my own experience last year, I wouldn't argue with that.

And now there is a new cadre of recruits to the ranks of the oppressed: immigrants. As an immigrant myself, I find this a bit baffling; but no doubt I am suffering from false consciousness.

The Huddled Masses: A New Surrogate Proletariat

Sentimental paternalism towards immigrants is by no means a new thing in U.S. history; nor is it, as sometimes claimed, an invention of the immigrants themselves. The impeccably blue-blooded WASP Jane Addams was being sentimental about immigrants in the 1880s.

That was, however, a Christian sentimentality joined to a desire to help people assimilate. Immigrants did not really become idols of the tribe until Cultural Marxism took hold in the 1960s.

The Hart-Celler immigration Act of 1965 already had a whiff of Cultural Marxism about it. One bit of true Marxism that survived into Cultural Marxism was the disdain for nations and nationhood. The abolition of national-origin quotas by the 1965 Act fitted very well with that; and if you read statements by the Act's supporters— Lyndon Johnson's speech at the signing ceremony, for example—you can see the swelling force of moral universalism lifting the whole thing up. The 1965 Act was widely seen, and soon became even more widely seen, as civil rights for foreigners—a *moral* issue.

And these foreigners were not shaped in any way by the nations, climates, religions, or races they came from. Perish the thought! They were, as Lyndon Johnson said, all Americans. They just had the misfortune not to have been born here—a misfortune easily rectified. The colonel in *Full Metal Jacket* expressed it in plainer language: "Inside every gook there is an American trying to get out."

The problem with this is that immigration is just a *policy*, like farm price supports or military procurements. It needs to be discussed calmly and rationally, with a fair weighing of pros and cons for the national interest.

It's hard to do that when an issue has been moralized. Opinions about the issue then become *not* correct or incorrect, *not* in or out of agreement with the data, *not* concordant or discordant with the national interest, but Good or Evil.

This didn't matter very much until the numbers of Third World immigrants had swollen to make them widely visible, taking over whole neighborhoods of our towns and cities. Being mainly nonwhite and former colonial subjects, these immigrants were easily romanticized as a new cohort of the surrogate proletariat—a new idol of the tribe.

As well as helping to fortify the new state ideology of Cultural Marxism, romanticization of Third World immigrants was mighty convenient to businessmen seeking cheap labor.

This had been a driving force for immigration in the Great Wave of the late 19th and early 20th century, leading to a reaction from the growing labor movement.

Here's a quote from a letter written in 1921: "Every citizen of the United States should make protest against the influx of people from other countries."

That was Samuel Gompers, President of the American Federation of Labor. The efforts of labor leaders like Gompers helped establish the 1924 Immigration Act, which greatly reduced numbers and formalized the national origins system.

By the late 20th century, though, the labor movement in the private sector had been gutted; and to the public sector, poor Third World immigrants were seen mainly as clients for government programs, requiring more government workers to minister to them, and therefore a benefit.

With labor opposition feeble, business was able freely to lobby and proselytize on behalf of more immigration, through mouthpieces like the *Wall Street Journal*. In a collaboration that would have astounded Marx himself, greedy capitalists had joined with his own intellectual descendants, as well as with the most important Christian and Jewish organizations, to abolish the nation-state.

The aim of the businessmen was of course was to depress wages, but the issue was never presented in these terms. Immigration had been thoroughly moralized and romanticized. Samuel Gompers was forgotten; so was the 1924 Act. The Statue of Liberty was no longer remembered to have been a gift from France to celebrate republican liberty and the American Revolution, but was widely believed—today

I think probably most Americans believe it—to be a monument to immigration.

And even as these malign forces were opening the nation's borders to entire vast new ethnies and races of settlers, our oldest race problem remained unsolved. The gulf between black and white Americans, which had shown some hopeful signs of narrowing in the middle 20th century, opened up wider and wider.

The Unbearable Whiteness of America: Misoleukanthropy

I first came to the U.S.A. in my late twenties, already an adult with a fairly solid set of working assumptions about the world. This put me in somewhat the position of an anthropologist observing a newly-discovered tribe.

One thing I noticed (and many others in similar circumstances have also noticed it—the historian John Lukacs, for example) was the plain hatred that many American blacks obviously felt towards whites. This didn't surprise me very much; given the history of slavery and Jim Crow, and the invariants of human nature, I suppose it's what one should expect. What *did* surprise me was the lengths to which white Americans go *not* to notice it.

White Americans who *did* betray the fact of having noticed suffered severe social ostracism. A case in point was journalist Amity Shlaes, who in January 1994 wrote an article titled *"Black Mischief"* for the London *Spectator*. In the article she described exactly what I had seen: the everyday hatred that black Americans nurse towards a white person like herself.

When this became known to Amity's colleagues at the *Wall Street Journal*, a deputation of them marched on the office of the chairman of Dow Jones, Inc., demanding that she be fired.

A few months later all the world got a good look at American blacks' hatred of whites when O.J. Simpson was acquitted of murdering his white wife, to scenes of wild rejoicing in black precincts.

Yet still white Americans mostly averted their eyes; and still today it is considered a gross breach of social etiquette to notice what a clear-eyed observer cannot help noticing.

Cultural Marxism seizes eagerly on this hatred, of course. So powerful is the ideology's appeal, in fact, that it has colonized the minds of the oppressors themselves, leaving them racked with guilt. Hence the phenomenon I call "ethnomasochism," by means of which white people too can savor the pleasure of hating whites.

Expressions of white ethnomasochism show up quite early on: Susan Sontag writing in 1967 that "The white race is the cancer of human history"; Stanley Ann Dunham around 1970 telling her Indonesian husband that American businessmen in Indonesia were "not my people"; Bill Clinton in 1998 saying that he looked forward to the day when whites will be a minority in America.

It is only recently, though, that hatred of whites has become a clear component of majority thinking, one of the idols of the tribe, out in the open for all to acknowledge and adore. Freshmen at our universities are now routinely put through training courses in which the white students among them are told of their own innate wickedness and warned that without a properly anti-white attitude, they will not be counted good citizens.

When the movie actor Jamie Foxx recently boasted on *Saturday Night Live* of having made a movie in which he gets to kill all the white people, the audience—which was almost entirely white—roared with laughter and approval. They love Big Brother.

It's easier to cope with and combat something if it has a name. I have been trying to come up with a snappier way of saying "hatred of whites," but the best I can do, drawing on a very scanty knowledge of classical Greek, is *misoluekanthropy*. I have not much hope this will catch on, but I offer it for your consideration anyway.

Once you are alert to misoleukanthropy you keep spotting new manifestations of it. There is an American pop singer named Beyoncé Knowles. I know next to nothing about pop music, which I pretty much gave up on after Buddy Holly died, but Ms. Knowles got my attention because my mother's surname was Knowles, so I could vaguely wonder if we were perhaps related.

Ms. Knowles, however, is racially what I think used to be called a "high yaller," or octoroon. The whiteness of her surname detracted somewhat from this. So she dropped the surname altogether and is now billed simply as Beyoncé, the horrid whiteness all purged out.

It's getting to be a common thing. There is a mulatto commentator on one of those leftist TV stations named Touré. That's it, just Touré—with, like Beyoncé, the acute accent for a touch of exoticism, of *authenticity*. If you look up Touré, you'll find that his surname is actually Neblett, which sounds even whiter than Knowles. Out, damn spot! Away with all whiteness!

What Is to Be Done?

I occasionally do some reading in neuroscience. Doing so a couple of years ago I came across a neurological affliction I had never heard of before: anosognosia.

Anosognosia is a condition in which the patient is suffering some severe neurological impairment *but does not know it*. The impairment is strictly neurological, in the higher processing regions of the brain. You might, for example, be suffering from paralysis of a limb, yet be unaware of it.

There are even some extreme cases recorded in which the sufferer is *blind* but does not know it! The eyes and optic nerves have normal function, but the brain centers that process visual stimulus are not working. To compensate, the brain *makes up* a visual field, trying to use cues from memory and the other senses.

It doesn't work very well. You keep falling over things, but *you can't understand why*.

Western society seems to have fallen into something like a social anosognosia. Our collective senses are gathering information OK, more than ever before in history in fact. But our collective brain is failing to process it, and compensates by making stuff up.

The Bureau of Labor Statistics and the Bureau of Justice Statistics, for example, do a great job as our sense organs, gathering important data that, if you process it in a straightforward way, tell you all you need to know about the bad effects of mass unskilled immigration, or race differentials in crime rates.

That processing, however, is not done.

For another example, consider Head Start, the program started in 1965—*1965!*—to improve the prospects for poor children by giving them pre-school education at federal expense. Every decade or so HHS does a study on the effectiveness of Head Start. Every study— the last one was published just before Christmas—says the same thing: that Head Start accomplishes nothing whatsoever.

If our collective brain were working properly, we'd dump the program. Instead, we just throw more money into it. In response to the latest HHS report, Congress *increased* funding for Head Start by $100m (by an item slipped into the Hurricane Sandy relief bill).

Wikipedia tells us that for anosognosia, "no long-term treatments exist." They do note, however, that *squirting ice cold water into the left ear* "is known to temporarily ameliorate unawareness of impairment."

That is our job here at *VDARE.com*: *to squirt cold water into society's left ear*. That's what we do here.

Thank you very much, ladies and gentlemen.

* * *

This article can be read online at http://www.vdare.com/articles/ john-derbyshire-s-address-to-the-first-vdarecom-webinar

A Modest Proposal on Politics and Intelligence

November 7, 2013

[This was an address delivered to the H.L. Mencken Club on Saturday, November 2, 2013. The theme of the weekend meeting was "Decadence"; the particular sub-theme we addressed on Saturday afternoon was "Political Decadence."]

Good afternoon, ladies and gentlemen. I am happy to see such a good turnout for this year's conference. I assume that no more than five or six of you can be moles from SPLC and the Cultural Marxist websites. [*VDARE.com* **note:** The SPLC had announced "[Derbyshire] plans to give a speech with the puzzlingly bland [*sic*] title, 'Politics and Intelligence.'" "White Nationalist Academics to Gather This Weekend for H.L. Mencken Club Annual Meeting," Ryan Lenz, *splcenter.org*, November 1, 2013.]

To them I say: Fie! To the rest of you: Welcome! to another gathering of the Dissident Right.

And that reminds me. Please excuse my doing a little promotion here.

You know how, when you leave home to go away for a couple of days, as you drive away you are nagged by the thought that you must have forgotten something? I was thus nagged as I left home on Thursday, and when I arrived here I realized that my inner nagger was operating on sound premises.

I saw the book table, and you can imagine me smacking myself on the forehead: I had forgotten to bring copies of my recent book, title *From the Dissident Right.* I apologize, although mostly to myself and my hungry family, for missing the opportunity to sell a few books, and I urge you to sprint away to your computers as soon as this session ends, to order a copy from the *VDARE.com* website, or from Amazon if you prefer.

All right, end of promotion. To the main topic: Politics and Intelligence.

When I saw the title of the topic, it rang a distant bell. Hadn't I written something about this once? I did a search on my archives. Sure enough, I turned up a piece I wrote for *National Review magazine* back in December of 2000, title: "Too Dumb to Vote."

On closer inspection, however, the opportunity was not such a great one. That column was…of its time. It was topical, inspired by the vote-count fiasco in Florida during the 2000 presidential election, which everyone now has forgotten about.

The heart of that matter was that George W. Bush came out ahead by a very slim margin in the original vote count, but there were a lot of spoiled ballots in several counties, and the Democratic challenger, Al Gore, demanded manual recounts.

The whole thing then went into the legal-constitutional weeds about how many recounts might be done, the deadlines for submitting the numbers, the recount process mechanics, and so on; and it ended up in the U.S. Supreme Court.

Here's a thing I wrote. You need to recall that the Governor of Florida at the time was Jeb Bush, a Republican.

When the Gore people asked for manual recounts in three of their counties, why didn't the Bush people do the same in three of theirs? Though I claim no inside knowledge, I am pretty sure I know the answer. The Bush people did not request recounts because they believed that any manual recount in *any* county would unearth extra Gore votes. They believed this because they believed that Republican voters do not mess up their ballot papers—not, at any rate, as often as Democrats do.…

For the Governor's people to say out loud that they believed the spoiling of ballots to be a mainly Democratic failing would be translated as: "GOP thinks Democrats are too dumb to vote." And that, in turn, would quickly be spun by the Democrats into: "GOP thinks African Americans are too dumb to vote." The Bush camp would rather be thought slow-footed than get stuck to *that* tar-baby. Being the Stupid Party isn't much fun, but in the minds of modern Republicans, it way beats being the Racist Party. ["Too Dumb to Vote," *National Review*, December 18, 2000.]

I went on to explore at some length the concept of being too dumb to vote. A lot of people *are* too dumb to vote, I don't think that can be doubted. That would include a lot of Democrats *and* a lot of Republicans. The number of Democrats who are too dumb to vote is likely greater, because the Democrats are the party of racial minorities with lower average IQs.

Worse than that, however: The proportion of too-dumb-to-vote Democrats who actually show up at the polls is *greater* than the corresponding proportion of too-dumb-to-vote Republicans. This is because of the different natures of the two parties' organizational histories. The Democrats are, always have been, better at rousing voters from their natural human condition of political apathy and busing them to the polls.

Taking the too-dumb-to-vote population as a whole, most of them, left to their own free choice, wouldn't *bother* to vote. Interest in politics is a fairly high-cognition function, not much found out on the left-hand tail of the Bell Curve. But the Democratic Party at the local level is expert at rousing these people from their beds of apathy and getting them to the polling station, sometimes with financial incentives as a spur. I don't say Republicans might not do this, but they don't do it half as much.

Regarding the too-dumb-to-vote demographic, it would be nice if we could contemplate a return of literacy tests for voting. They used to be very common: Some parts of New York State had them as late as 1970. There's a common belief that the 1965 Voting Rights Act outlawed them. In fact it didn't, but it put voting requirements under federal surveillance, and that killed off literacy tests just as effectively as if they *had* been explicitly outlawed.

I don't know—although I bet my friend Bob Weissberg knows—whether literacy tests have ever actually been declared unconstitutional. I can't see why they should be. Many of our constitutional rights can be exercised only after jumping through some procedural and administrative hoops. In my own state of New York, for instance, the right to own a handgun depends on your having passed through a lengthy process of inquiry into your character and habits, carried out by the local police.

As I said, it would be nice if we could contemplate a return of literacy tests. In our present cultural milieu, however, this is beyond unthinkable, so I won't dwell on it.

And the too-dumb-to-vote segment is only a part of the problem we conservatives have with universal suffrage. Here's another part: too *smart* to vote.

People of very high intelligence are especially susceptible to large abstract theories about society. Those of a literary inclination fall for romantic and imaginative theories like those identified by Stephen Pinker: illusions about the Noble Savage, the Blank Slate, and the Ghost in the Machine. Mathematical and scientific types are prone to see politics in terms of engineering; to see human populations as quantities of concrete to be shoveled around. As P.J. O'Rourke said after visiting Poland in the 1970s: "Commies *love* concrete."

In my 2000 article I proposed the following counterfactual thought experiment:

> Suppose that in, say, 1920 the U.S. franchise had been limited to citizens holding a Ph.D. What would the consequences have been? Is there any doubt that we should have had a Soviet America in very short order, and that we should right now be digging ourselves out of the same pit the poor Russians find themselves in?

Political stupidity is in fact a *special kind* of stupidity, not well correlated with other kinds. Think of the barmy political programs that issued forth, with such confidence, from Jean-Paul Sartre, Bertrand Russell, Norman Mailer and other members of the mid-20th-century preposterentsia, as exposed in withering detail in Paul Johnson's book *Intellectuals*.

At the very highest levels of intelligence, the correlation between IQ and sensible political opinions may actually be *inverse*: the more brilliant you are, the dumber your politics. Albert Einstein thought well of Stalin; Hitlerism got its first mass following in the highly-selective German universities.

In my book *Prime Obsession*, which is about the history of a certain mathematical topic, I passed the following remark about the German university town of Göttingen, the beating heart of high mathematical excellence from the early 19th century to the mid-20th. Quote:

> Göttingen at large was rather strong for Hitler. This was true of both "town" and "gown." In the 1930 elections, Göttingen had delivered twice as many votes to Hitler's party as the national average; and the Nazis had a majority in the university's student congress as far back as 1926.

There is in fact a sort of Goldilocks Principle here. In the 2012 election, voters who did not graduate from high school went 63 percent for Obama. High school graduates with no college, 51 percent. Some college, but not a full 4-year degree: 49 percent. College graduates overall: 47 percent. Then the porridge gets warm again: holders of postgraduate degrees: 55 percent. ["Exit polls 2012: How the Vote Has Shifted," *Washington Post*, November 6, 2012.]

At even higher intellectual levels, I'm sure the porridge is even warmer. I live a mile or two from Cold Spring Harbor lab, which employs a lot of extremely smart biologists and geneticists. A neighbor of mine who works there told me at the time of the 1994 mid-term sweep by Republican candidates for Congress that his fellow researchers were, quote, "all in tears" about it.

Thus the relationship between intelligence and politics follows the old Anglo-Saxon model of class warfare: the top and the bottom united against the middle.

In the English Civil War of the 1640s, town-dwellers, merchants, artisans, and other people of what at the time was called "the middle kind" took up arms against a coalition of the top and the bottom.

At the top were the Stuart King and the older, more traditional component of the aristocracy, many of whom had remained Catholic. They united with poorer elements of the peasantry, many of whom had likewise remained Catholic.

In the craggy, stony, upland parts of the kingdom, where the poorest people lived, Royalist sentiment was especially strong. As Kevin Phillips notes in his book *The Cousins' Wars*

Support for King Charles also predominated in the higher elevations of Derbyshire.

There were of course some exceptions. The university towns, for example, went different ways: Oxford staunchly Royalist, while Cambridge—where, after all, Oliver Cromwell had attended college—was mainly for Parliament.

The Goldilocks pattern was the norm, though. It continued into British electoral politics, when there began to be such a thing in its modern form.

The poorest classes of the 18th century had no vote, but the petty gentry of the shires—people like Squire Western in *Tom Jones*, who were regarded as uncouth boors by townspeople—voted Tory and were strong for the monarchy and the Established church, while the bourgeoisie and most of the intelligentsia (Dr. Johnson the notable exception) were Whigs.

The same pattern showed up over here in the War Between the States, with the Union drawing its main strength from commercially-minded townspeople and artisans, while the Confederacy depended more on wealthy planters and traditionalist country people, small farmers of old colonial stock like the Georgia crackers.

I intend no prejudice to the English Royalists or the Confederacy, with both of which I have some sympathy (but both of whom, I am bound to note, lost). In any case, so far as social class is concerned, the post-WW2 rise of the meritocracy has turned the Goldilocks Principle inside-out. Error and folly are now found among the top-and-bottom alliance much more than in the sensible middle.

I suggest therefore that there may be a "sweet spot" for fruitful political participation somewhere around the middle of the IQ range, or at any rate away from the extremes.

My modest proposal for improving our political life would therefore be to remove from the voter rolls all persons of too low or too high intelligence.

I'll leave it to our constitutional experts to decide where the cutoff should be. If we put it at two standard deviations from the mean, we'd be excluding four percent of the voting-age population. At one standard deviation, we'd be excluding 32 percent, which would be more to my liking.

Dumb people are a burden society has to bear in a spirit of Christian charity and patriotic solidarity. Many of them are our friends, relatives, and bosses. So: "He ain't heavy, he's my brother." Smart people are a nuisance and a menace if they are allowed to meddle too much in public affairs.

The political stability of a society depends on its intellectual *ballast*—the stolid, practical, unimaginative middle: people smart enough to manage their own lives independently and to calculate the general interest, but not so smart as to fall for romantic follies or inhuman schemes of social engineering.

Let's exclude the rest!

Thank you, ladies and gentlemen!

* * *

This article can be read online at http://www.vdare.com/articles/ john-derbyshire-s-modest-proposal-on-politics-and-intelligence

VDare Articles

Today's Forgotten Men—The American White Working Class

January 31, 2013

The other day I mentioned former *Wall Street Journal* editorial-page editor Amity Shlaes in connection with her 1994 piece "Black Mischief" in the London *Spectator*. Ms. Shlaes has a new book coming out a week next Tuesday, a biography of Calvin Coolidge. I'll be reviewing it here on *VDARE.com* (see p. 39).

Ms. Shlaes is probably best known for her 2009 libertarian-contrarian account of the Great Depression, *The Forgotten Man.* She borrowed her title from an 1883 essay by classical liberal William Graham Sumner. The Forgotten Man is the hapless middle- or working-class schmuck who ends up paying for the grand schemes of social improvement foisted on a nation by politicians, political entrepreneurs, ideologues, and do-gooders.

I liked the book well enough, but I liked the title even more. Sumner had identified an enduring truth about modern democratic society. There is at every time some group of persons, in some kind of pickle—"some man or group of men whose case appeals to the sympathies and the imagination" (Sumner)—on whom politicians and the media shine the benevolent light of their countenances, vowing to take measures to relieve that group of its troubles. And there is another group of persons, barely noticed or mentioned, and including *no members at all* of the light-shining classes, who will be stuck with the price of that relief, to their great disadvantage. Those are the Forgotten Men.

This came to mind as I was reading Wednesday's *New York Post*. Although a sensibly conservative paper on many important topics—law-enforcement, public finances, fracking, the "human rights" rackets, the evil of public-sector unions—the *NYP* is clueless on immigration. In Wednesday's issue, it is editorializing about "bringing in from the cold the 11 million illegals already here and instituting a guest-

27

worker program." ["Immigration: Fix It!" January 30, 2013.] Any regular *VDARE.com* reader can take an axe to these weary clichés: eleven million is surely an underestimate, we already have visa categories for every conceivable type of guest worker, etc.

It was, however, not the *NYP*'s editorial pages that got me thinking about the Forgotten Man, but the news pages. It covered Barack Obama's speech in Las Vegas, as of course it should have done; but it decorated its coverage with three "case studies" to illustrate the problem the President claimed to be addressing. ["Obama's Immigration 'Campaign'," Geoff Earle, January 30, 2013.]

- Case Study #1: Martha Guolotuna, owner of an autobody shop (apparently a clean one) in the borough of Queens, who "departed Quito, Ecuador, for a new life in the United States 18 years ago."

- Case Study #2: Yenny Quispe, occupation not given, who "has been in America for 10 years after fleeing Peru with her mother and brother to escape her abusive father."

- Case Study #3: Tania Gordillo, apparently unemployed, who "came to the United States in 1995 from Ecuador and learned what it's like to be undocumented."

The main impression these thumbnail "case studies" give is a whiny sense of entitlement. Ms. Guolotuna wants to "be treated like everyone else." Ms. Quispe has "been waiting a long time." (Though not as long as a Family First Preference visa applicant from the Philippines, which currently requires an 11-year wait—in, of course, the Philippines. For a Fourth Preference Filipino/a the wait time is *19 years*.) Ms. Gordillo is "tired of constantly looking over my shoulder."

Remedies for her fatigue come easily to mind. Has our domestic production of I'm-entitled whiners really fallen so low we need to import?

And entirely left out of the *Post* story is the Forgotten Man. Could it not have included just *one* case study of an American who has been disadvantaged by our government's long failure to enforce the people's laws on immigration?

Of course, it could, and there are some obvious examples one might bring forward: for example, Danielle Bologna, in hiding after being deprived of her husband and two sons by an MS-13 gangster.

To be fair to the *Post*, though, there is a fundamental difficulty here, the one William Graham Sumner identified.

Dramatic cases like that of poor Mrs. Bologna aside, the Forgotten Man is forgotten for a very understandable reason: the cost to him of bad policies accumulates slowly, imperceptibly, spread across millions of others like him. He is the proverbial frog being proverbially boiled. At the end of the process he is, like the frog, considerably worse off; but at no point did the gentle downward trajectory in his fortunes jar him into defensive action...or excite the sympathies of politicians or *Post* reporters.

In the matter of our foolish immigration policies, and our government's failure to enforce them even in all their foolishness, the Forgotten Man is the working-class American: the adult citizen who must put in forty hours of more of drudge work every week in order to maintain a home and feed a family, or the teenager seeking money and work experience in his school summer vacation.

The adult citizen's wages have stagnated or declined; the teenager has no recollection of a happier time to compare with.

That mass immigration depresses working-class wages is obvious, and well-documented. Surveying the economic history of the U.S.A. in the 20th century, it is tempting to see it all Marxistly as a long conspiracy by Capital to keep down the price of labor.

There was the Great Wave of European immigration that petered off in WW1, then ended decisively with the 1924 Immigration Act. By that time, though, the Great Migration of rural blacks from the

South was under way, keeping up the supply of cheap factory labor until the Depression, which ended with WW2.

The 20 years following WW2 are looked back on by nostalgists of the Pat Buchanan stripe as a golden age for U.S. labor, with well-paying jobs for all able-bodied citizens (including even a second phase of the Great Migration). This, our Marxist-conspiracist might argue, was an anomaly, defying gravity by virtue of other advanced nations being in ruins, or trapped in Communism. Downward pressure on working wages was re-asserted with the 1965 Immigration Act, and median family income has been basically flat since the early 1970s.

I am temperamentally skeptical of conspiracy theories myself. But looking at the legions of billionaires bankrolling both parties' campaigns in November, one can't help but be suspicious.

The frog-boiling process may have been gradual enough to keep the working class peaceful, but it has left them mightily disgruntled.

Least gruntled of all are white non-Hispanic workers, who in addition to seeing their wages stagnate or decline have been insulted by race preferences ("Affirmative Action") and disproportionately shut out from government jobs, which have been fenced off as a make-work reservation for low-ability minorities.

The consequences were plain to see in last November's election. The white working class, seeing nothing to hope for from either party's presidential candidate, stayed home.

The interesting question here is why, in an open and democratic society, such a large quantity of disgruntlement has found no political expression.

The most depressing explanation—and so naturally the one I favor—is despair. The white working class understands that the game is up for them. They are the Forgotten Men, and they know it.

It has long been an article of faith with economists that as technology changes the labor market, it always does so in such a way that more jobs are created than lost: the redundant blacksmith opens an autobody shop, and so on. (Let's hope he doesn't find himself competing with Ms. Guolotuna.)

This is not *necessarily* so, however. It is not a physical principle built in to the structure of reality, like the Laws of Thermodynamics. It has just always been the case. To suppose it will go on being the case may be an instance of extrapolation bias. In fact there are signs we may have reached, or passed, Peak Jobs—that jobs are now being destroyed faster than they are being created.

It may be that the white working class know this in their bones, and have just given up. After forty years of relentless downward pressure on wages under administrations of both parties, with welfare an increasingly attractive alternative to employment weighed down with swelling taxes and health-care bills, with entertainment and political elites ever more arrogant in contempt for them; it may be that the white working class has sunk into irredeemable apathy.

They may even believe they are drifting into a future of the Frederick Pohl or Neal Stephenson type, where most work has disappeared, only a small elite have jobs, and the non-elite masses are kept pacified with welfare, low-grade entertainment, and robot-produced consumer goods.

The fate of the current Open-Borders efforts by Congress and the President will be a test of this apathy theory. If indeed the white working classes are so demoralized and passive that they will accept this further insult to them, to their livelihoods, and to their children's future, then we shall indeed have "comprehensive immigration reform" and the inevitable following surge of tens of millions more cheap workers.

If, on the other hand, there is a successful 2007-style push-back against "reform," then there is life in the American white working class yet. And we sad augurs will mock our own presage.

If—though this may be too much to hope for—if, in addition, there were to be just one big, noisy demonstration by non-Hispanic whites, preferably with a few windows broken in government offices,

I might even believe that the war against the white working class that has been going on all over the Western world this past forty years, might be entering a new, more hopeful, phase.

Aux armes, citoyens!

* * *

This article can be read online at http://www.vdare.com/articles/ john-derbyshire-on-today-s-forgotten-men-the-american-white- working-class

On State of the Union Signals—Is Obama's Immigration Enthusiasm Waning?

February 13, 2013

In *We Are Doomed* I referred to the State of the Union address as a "Stalinesque extravaganza."

> You know how it goes. We're shown the House chamber, where the nation's highest civilian and military officials wait in gathering expectation. The Sergeant at Arms announces the President's arrival. The great man appears at last. In his progress through the chamber, legislators jostle and maneuver to catch his eye and receive the favor of a presidential greeting.
>
> On the podium at last, the President offers up preposterously grandiose assurances of protection, provision, and moral guidance from his government, these declarations of benevolent omnipotence punctuated by standing ovations and cheers from legislators of his own party, and often from the others too, after every declarative clause.

Things haven't improved any in the four years since I wrote that. Every year grows stronger my yearning for a return to the modest style that prevailed through most of the Republic's history, of the President delivering a written report to Congress on the State of the Union. Vain hope, of course: the politicians of this age don't do modest.

Well, well, what did the President have to tell us about the State of our Union? On the topic that most concerns readers of *VDARE.com*, next to nothing: there was less than 2½ minutes on immigration in a one-hour speech, and this came at well past the halfway mark, when many viewers will have given up.

Opener:

33

"Our economy is stronger when we harness the talents and ingenuity of striving, hopeful immigrants [applause]; and right now, leaders of business, labor, law enforcement, faith communities, they all agree that the time has come to pass comprehensive immigration reform [prolonged applause]."

Mostly true. Business leaders have no problem with private-sector labor markets being flooded to bring down wages. "Labor" nowadays means public-sector employees, to whom immigrants are clients, i.e. bread and butter. "Faith communities," formerly known as churches, are in the nation-wrecking van of immigration romanticism and refugee resettlement, to the disgust of many patriotic congregants.

"Law enforcement" needs some qualification, however, with one leader in that field testifying to Congress recently that his officers are disciplined for arresting illegal immigrants.

In confirmation of that testimony, there were illegal immigrants *sitting right there in the House chamber* as the President spoke, brought in as guests of congressmen. Why did not the Capitol police arrest them?

So perhaps not quite *all* leaders agree. And what about followers? Oh, the heck with *them!*

What exactly *is* comprehensive immigration reform, though? Let the President tell us:

"Real reform means stronger border security, and we can build on the progress my administration's already made, putting more boots on the southern border than at any time in our history...."

There flashed upon my inward eye at that point a stretch of southern border desert country with thousands of empty boots laid out on it in a line stretching all the to the horizon. Perhaps that's what the President has in mind, who knows?

"…and reducing illegal crossings to their lowest levels in forty years…."

Really? Great! So we can reassign Border Patrol agents to internal enforcement, right, Mr. President? Mr. President? Hello?

"…a responsible pathway to earned citizenship, a path that includes passing a background check, paying taxes and a meaningful penalty, learning English, and going to the back of the line behind folks trying to come here legally [applause]."

That would presumably be the line that is, for some categories of legal immigrants, nineteen years long.

"And real reform means fixing the legal immigration system…."

Whoa! A politician talking about fixing *legal* immigration! Fixing which aspect? Chain migration? The diversity lottery? Birthright citizenship? So much needs fixing!

"…to cut waiting periods and attract the highly skilled entrepreneurs and engineers that will help create jobs and grow our economy [prolonged applause]."

Oh. I guess there are not, among us 310 million American citizens, enough with engineering skills and entrepreneurial zip to keep the show going. What a sad lot we are, we Americans!

"In other words, we know what needs to be done…." Yes, yes, we all know! There is no disagreement! [Applause. Standing applause. All stand. Standing ovation.]

That was it. On what the President had formerly declared would be one of the foremost initiatives of his administration, only a handful of weary clichés and semi-truths slipped in between "schools worthy of our children" and a promise to raise the minimum wage.

For some listeners, they weren't even the right clichés. From that *USA Today* report on invited illegals, these particular ones in a House committee room, not the chamber:

> Eric Rodriguez, 30, the son of illegal immigrants who became citizens after the last large-scale immigration law passed in 1986, said he was disturbed that Obama only singled out immigrants with high-tech degrees. "By him focusing on highly skilled immigrants, you completely disregard this whole room," said Rodriguez, who runs the Latino Union of Chicago, which organizes domestic workers and day laborers. ["Some Attending Obama Speech Are in the U.S. Illegally," Alan Gomez, February 13, 2013.]

Because, you know, what the U.S.A. *really* needs is more domestic workers and day laborers.

Would it be wildly optimistic to read into the President's cursory treatment of immigration some sign of his backing off the subject? Obama is too skillful a politician to yoke himself to a hopeless cause. Is he having doubts? Are the congressional switchboards lighting up already? One can only hope.

The rest of the speech was hot air. If there is any purpose to the President addressing Congress in person, it would be to expose points of failure in areas where the legislature and executive are supposed to co-operate. Current examples would include the Senate's disgraceful failure to pass a national budget in four years, and the Office of Refugee Resettlement's delinquency, also now four years long, in not submitting annual reports to Congress as required by law.

There was nothing of that, only self-congratulatory gas about having "cleared away the rubble of crisis" and promises to eradicate world poverty, as if that were possible, or any of our business.

Marco Rubio, in the official GOP response to Obama, also skipped lightly over immigration.

"We can also help grow our economy if we have a legal immigration system that allows us to attract and assimilate the world's best and brightest. We need a responsible permanent solution to the problem of those who are here illegally. But first we must follow through on the broken promises of the past, to secure our borders and enforce our laws."

That was it: 21 seconds in a 15-minute speech, with a leaning to enforcement and border security. Possibly Rubio was saving his immigration enthusiasm for the Spanish-language version of his response. *VDARE.com* has Alan Wall listening to that, so you will be told. [*VDARE.com* **note:** *Allan Wall said that Rubio said the same thing in English and Spanish, which is better than George Bush's official translators could do in 2004.*]

There was a second response from Senator Rand Paul on behalf of the Tea Party movement. On immigration, Paul was easily the most depressing of the three speakers.

"We must be the party that sees immigrants as assets."

Well, that's a tad better than seeing them as voting-booth fodder (Obama) or cheap labor (Conservatism, Inc.) But:

"If you want to work, if you want to be in America, we welcome you."

All five billion of you, presumably. I refer Senator Paul to my "Libertarianism in One Country" column, though without much hope: I concluded some time ago that libertarians are, on the National Question, radically hopeless.

Thus another annual Stalinesque extravaganza fades into the mist. Did I really see Janet Napolitano kiss Elena Kagan? Perhaps I imag-

ined it. Did I really hear Barack Obama call for "not a bigger government but a smarter government"? Yes, that one I have in my notes.
But then, some years ago at a different President's SOTU, I heard that
"the era of big government is over."

If only the era of spoken SOTUs would be over and the era of
written ones—Jefferson to Taft—restored.

* * *

This article can be read online at http://www.vdare.com/articles/
sotu-signals-is-obamas-immigration-enthusiasm-waning

On Amity Shlaes on Calvin Coolidge: Why So Little Mention of the 1924 Immigration Act?

February 21, 2013

Perhaps as a reaction to the morbidly obese statism of early 21st-century U.S. federal governments, there is a modest upswell of interest in Calvin Coolidge, who of all presidents in the previous century was the most dogged and unwavering in pursuit of lower federal expenditures and debt.

Last week saw the publication of Amity Shlaes' *Coolidge*, which I have just been reading. Next month comes Charles C. Johnson's *Why Coolidge Matters: Leadership Lessons from America's Most Underrated President*, which I have not yet seen. The main subject of this column will be Ms. Shlaes' book. (Full disclosure: I am the author of a novel titled *Seeing Calvin Coolidge in a Dream*.)

Coolidge was Warren Harding's Vice President. He succeeded to the presidency on Harding's sudden death in August, 1923. Coolidge and his wife were vacationing at the time in the remote Vermont farming hamlet where he had been raised. The thirtieth president was sworn in by his father, a notary public, in Coolidge, Sr.'s living-room, by the light of a kerosene lamp—electricity had not yet reached the village.

Coolidge served out Harding's term, then easily won a term of his own in a three-way contest elegantly described by Garland Tucker in his book *The High Tide of American Conservatism*. But, although successful and popular, Coolidge declined to run for a second full term in 1928, for reasons that remain opaque in spite of his having given over eight pages of his autobiography to "explaining" them.

Amity Shlaes' book concentrates on Coolidge's budgetary and fiscal policies, which were very astute, and delivered great prosperity and social peace. This all built on foundations laid by Harding, who had created a Budget Bureau (now the OMB) and settled the budget process in the form we still use today, more or less, via the Budget and Accounting Act of 1921.

The first Director of the Budget Bureau was Charles G. Dawes, later Coolidge's Vice President. Dawes—if you are conservative, prepare to swoon—created a Federal Liquidation Board: "an entity whose entire purpose [Ms. Shlaes tells us] was to shutter government and military offices."

Be still, my heart!

Coolidge continued these policies of federal reduction to such a point that his success generated problems of its own. Just as the trick of being a medieval monarch was to leave behind a healthy heir, but not more than one, so the trick of federal budget management is to generate a surplus that is *not too big*. Ms. Shlaes, writing about the beginning of Coolidge's presidency: "Voters wanted the federal government to spend, and lawmakers were ready to help."

Some things don't change.

Shlaes writes all this up decently, and an author is of course entitled to choose her own approach and make her own emphases. Followers of *VDARE.com*, however, will naturally want to know: what has she to say about Coolidge's attitude to the epochal Immigration Act of 1924, which was aimed at reducing immigrant numbers and preserving the nation's ethnic balance?

Answer: *Not much*. In aggregate, a little over one page in 461 pages of narrative.

Given the momentous demographic consequences of the Act, of which more in a moment, this must be regarded as unforgivably dismissive.

I suppose you could argue: since Coolidge played no part in initiating, promoting, or moving the Act; since he had only been President for a few weeks when the 68th Congress began debating the Act (at that point of course merely a bill); since the Act generated little controversy at the time outside special-interest factions (the House voted for it 306-58, the Senate 69-9); and since Coolidge's few remarks on immigration, for example in his 1923 State of the Union address, were blandly consensual—which is to say, favorable (in that enlightened era) to patriotic immigration reform—no lengthy discussion of the topic is appropriate in a Coolidge biography.

Maybe. But what would qualify as "lengthy"? Let's compare Ms. Shlaes' aggregate page-and-a-quarter with coverage by Coolidge's other biographers.

Coolidge's own account of his life and career is, as usual, perfectly unhelpful. His book is in fact a strong contender for the title Least Revealing Autobiography Ever Written. [Read it online at Archive.org.] Some serious observers have expressed the belief that the whole thing is one of Coolidge's dry, subtle jokes, written with the intention to discover the absolute minimum it is possible to say in 245 pages. Had I been Marketing Manager for the Cosmopolitan Book Corporation in 1929, I would have sold the *Autobiography* with the promise of a $1,000 prize for anyone who could prove he had stayed awake while reading it:

> It is a very old saying that you never can tell what you can do until you try. The more I see of life the more I am convinced of the wisdom of that observation.... (p. 171)

Claude M. Fuess's 1939 biography *Calvin Coolidge, The Man from Vermont,* which is every Coolidgean's favorite for its literate, sympathetic, and historically well-informed portrait of the man, *does not mention the Immigration Act at all.* ("Fuess" is pronounced to rhyme with "peace." He was George H.W. Bush's headmaster at Andover.) Even when discussing allied topics—labor leader Samuel Gompers, for example, who was of course a keen supporter of the 1924 Act—Fuess has nothing to say on immigration.

Donald McCoy's *Calvin Coolidge: The Quiet President* (1967) gives the most thorough coverage of the Act: five full pages out of 422. But four of those five concern the knotty but minor issue of Japanese exclusion.

Japanese immigration had been vexing the West Coast in the early 1900s. It was defused at last by Theodore Roosevelt with a "gentlemen's agreement" under which the Japanese authorities would no longer issue passports to U.S.-bound emigrants, in return for U.S. acceptance of Japanese already settled here.

Coolidge thought this executive-to-executive agreement dealt adequately with Japanese immigration, and that the specific exclusion clause in the 1924 Act was not only unnecessary, but would be taken as an insult by the "face"-conscious Japanese.

And it was: in fact, the Japanese over-reacted, thereby stirring up Senatorial resentment in counter-reaction, and Coolidge lost his fight to have the exclusion clause modified.

Unwilling to veto the Act, to which he was otherwise sympathetic, Coolidge signed it on May 26, 1924, attaching a statement that he thought the Japanese exclusion clause "unnecessary and deplorable at this time."

It's a bit of a stretch to argue, as McCoy does, that the 1924 Act's exclusion clause contributed to the rise of Japanese militarism in the 1930s. But the executive-legislative tussle over the clause was, if not a political hurricane, at least a gale, and should certainly be covered in a Coolidge biography.

The late Bob Sobel, in his 1998 book *Coolidge: An American Enigma* echoes McCoy:

Relations with the Japanese deteriorated. It was another step on the road to war.

For goodness sake! It's bad enough that Cal gets blamed (absurdly in my opinion, and Ms. Shlaes seems to agree) for the Great Depression. Do we have to pin Pearl Harbor on him, too?

David Greenberg, writing the Coolidge volume for Times Books' "American Presidents" series (my review at http://www.john derbyshire.com/Reviews/History/calvincoolidge.html), goes even further. After 2½ pages of mildly tendentious coverage of the Immigration Act ("a nativist movement had arisen"; the Act's "barely disguised racism"; etc.), Greenberg emits this [square brackets all mine]:

> [Coolidge] signed the bill, Japanese exclusion and all, on May 26. As a result, only a tiny number of immigrants would enter the United States over the next four decades, profoundly affecting the demographic and political character of the nation. [!] After the Holocaust of the 1930s and '40s, the bill would come to be seen [by whom?] as a betrayal of the nation's promise [made when? to whom?] of an open door—one that, along with its other unfortunate effects [such as?], helped consign millions of European Jews to death. Not until a major new immigration law was passed in 1965 would America's doors open again.

The Great Depression, Pearl Harbor, the Holocaust...I suppose we should be grateful that so far nobody has blamed Coolidge for the Death of Vaudeville.

Amity Shlaes covers the issue of the Japanese exclusion clause very briskly, in three non-contiguous sentences. She tells us that Coolidge conceded on it in order to concentrate his strength behind Andrew Mellon's tax plan.

I think this is plausible. (And I note, with another flutter of the heart, that in April, the month before Coolidge signed the Immigration Act, the Treasury planned a Tax Reduction Week to publicize Mellon's proposals. When will the republic again celebrate a Tax Reduction Week? Perhaps around the same time we see another Federal Liquidation Board.)

For *VDARE.com* readers who want to know more about the Japanese exclusion clause, the best coverage known to me is in Chapter Seven of Kevin MacDonald's *Culture of Critique*. MacDonald has an argument to make, which you may agree or disagree with, but he has at least actually read the *Congressional Record* for the relevant dates, and deftly fillets later smug propaganda about "racism" and "supremacy" as important driving forces behind the exclusion clause:

> Several restrictionists explicitly denounced the theory of Nordic superiority, including [long list of congresscritters]. Indeed, it is noteworthy that there are indications in the congressional debate that representatives from the far West were concerned about the competence and competitive threat presented by Japanese immigrants, and their rhetoric suggests they viewed the Japanese as racially equal or superior, not inferior. For example, Senator Jones stated, "We admit that [the Japanese] are as able as we are, that they are as progressive as we are, that they are as honest as we are, and that they are equal in all that goes to make a great people and nation"…and Representative Lea noted their ability to supplant "their American competitor."

The Japanese issue aside, Ms. Shlaes has almost nothing to say about the Immigration Act. In the little she does say, while at least sparing us overt Greenbergian piffle about "nativism," she none the less manages to offer a glimpse of open-borders ankle:

> Senator William Dillingham…had fought hard to restrict immigration in the past and plotted yet more immigration law now.

"Plotted"? That's a fine word for a polemic, but out of place in a political biography. Dillingham—a Vermonter, like Coolidge—was no backstairs political plotter, but a heavyweight statesman and long-dedicated immigration patriot, who had chaired the 1907-10 United States Immigration Commission and supervised production of its massively-detailed 41-volume report.

Like Moses, he saw the Promised Land, but was not permitted to enter therein: He died in July 1923, a few months before Coolidge signed the Immigration Act.

Again:

Coolidge was willing to go along with restrictionists. "I am convinced that our present economic and social conditions warrant a limitation of those to be admitted," he wrote. But he was not hostile to immigrants already in the United States.

Why should anyone think he was? Because we should assume, in the infantile schoolyard mentality of our wretched time, that immigration restrictionism is a species of "Hate"?

I repeat: Ms. Shlaes is entitled to her own approach and emphases, and her coverage of the 1924 Act is around the median for the other five biographies I have mentioned. Other than signing the Act and lobbying for some deference to Japanese sensitivities, Coolidge had very little to do with it.

The lapses of logic and sense I have noted in *Coolidge* are anyway plucked straight from the loathsome *Zeitgeist*, with perhaps some additional motivation from the abrasions the author suffered nineteen years ago when she crashed the boundaries of America's peculiar racial decorum.

Coolidge is not a bad read. Still, David Greenberg made the key point, though not in the way he intended.

The 1924 Immigration Act did indeed profoundly affect the demographic and political character of the nation, by creating—with some later assistance from Presidents F. D. Roosevelt, Truman, and Eisenhower—a forty-year immigration moratorium in which was forged the strongest, happiest, most prosperous, and most culturally vibrant nation the world has ever seen.

The President who signed that Act did much else that was good. But historians of a century or two from now, if there are any, will place that signing, not fiscal fiddling and budgetary bafflegab, at the top when they list Calvin Coolidge's accomplishments.

* * *

This article can be read online at http://www.vdare.com/articles/ john-derbyshire-on-amity-shlaes-on-calvin-coolidge-why-so-little- mention-of-the-1924-immigr

Jeb Bush Just Doesn't Like Americans Very Much

March 7, 2013

As you read through a book, as the pages clock by, hints of the author's underlying attitudes accumulate until, by halfway through the thing, you have a clear picture of those attitudes. In the case of a certain type of author—a person with not much power of imagination or self-examination—you may have a clearer picture of his attitudes than he has himself.

So with *Immigration Wars*, the new book by Jeb Bush and Clint Bolick. I just got through reading the book on Kindle: the square brackets in what follows refer to locations in the Kindle text.

Yes, there are two authors there, and you can speculate for yourself about who did how much of the writing. But, given that Jeb Bush is an ambitious politician, and that now is about the right time for ambitious politicians to lay down markers for the 2016 election, I doubt there is a single sentence here that Jeb Bush didn't sign off on—whether he actually wrote the book or not. So I am blaming him for it.

So what insights into this possible 2016 presidential candidate do we get from *Immigration Wars*?

The main one I got: *Jeb Bush just doesn't like Americans very much.*

Immigration boosterism always has a whiff of this about it. "Jobs Americans won't do"—*because they are too spoiled and lazy!* "Skill shortages"—*resulting from Americans being too dumb!*

Bush packs both of those into a single sentence:

It is essential that we have an ample supply of workers both for labor-intensive jobs that few Americans want and for highly skilled jobs for which there are inadequate numbers of Americans with the skills to fit them. [1207]

Business-wise we're not up to much, either: "Like most immigrants, Hispanics are tremendously entrepreneurial." [2206] *As opposed to those dull, risk-averse non-Hispanic and non-immigrant
Americans!*

As *VDARE.com* readers know, this last assertion is demonstrably
untrue. Indeed, Bush's book abounds in long-debunked falsehoods—
so much so that, by fifty or so pages in, the well-informed commentator can't resist doing a search on "44 percent." Yep, there it is!—
"Whereas Republicans had won 44 percent of the Hispanic vote...."
[2067]

When not telling outright porkies, Jeb Bush offers assertions su-
perficially friendly to his case, while omitting taboo-related explanatory factors:

El Paso, Texas, is one of the nation's three largest safe cities.
[990]

Yes, because the black population is unusually low: 2.8 percent, only
a tad higher than Salt Lake City's 2.5 percent.

The deficiencies of us actual citizens of the U.S.A. are even *spiri-
tual.*

Immigrants are unlikely to be complacent about the freedom
and opportunity that for them previously was only a dream
and was gained only through great effort and sacrifice. Our nation constantly needs the replenishment of our spirit that immigrants bring. [834]

The accumulating impression left by Jeb Bush: Americans are not
much good for anything. Only immigrants, with "their energy, vitality, talent, and enterprise" [992] can overcome the lassitude, torpor,
mediocrity, and complacency of the native-born.

We get a revealing metaphor here, one that puts me in mind of old
Soviet propaganda movies:

When immigration policy is working right, it is like a hydro-electric dam: a sturdy wall who valves allow torrents of water to pour through, creating massive amounts of dynamic energy. [202]

Presumably that is energy that we dull natives could not possibly generate on our own.

How on earth did the nation cope under the low-immigration regime of the 1950s?

How did New England survive *two centuries* of essentially zero immigration (1640s to 1840s)?

Our failures extend into the reproductive zone:

America's birthrate has fallen below the level needed to replace the current population. [897]

To keep our welfare programs going, says Jeb Bush, we need a steady flow of immigrants.

The counters to *that* are well-known to anyone decently well-read in immigration topics. The best-known counter includes the phrase "Ponzi scheme."

And then there is Mark Krikorian in his 2008 book *The New Case Against Immigration*, observing that American birthrates might increase if immigration were to be curtailed.

Economist Richard Easterlin has long argued that one of the causes of the postwar Baby Boom was the higher wages young people were able to earn at the time because of the tight labor market caused by restricted immigration. (*Op. cit.*, p. 199)

As Mark notes, Steve Sailer's "affordable family formation" theory is also relevant here.

So Jeb Bush's view of the American people has us always trending towards a condition of listless, ignorant, complacent, unentrepreneurial, non-reproducing sloth—unless continuously energized by floods of immigrants. As I began by saying, *he just doesn't much like us very much.*

Isn't it unwise of an ambitious politician to reveal that much about himself to the public?

Why would any American vote for a man who holds us in such contempt?

It can't be that Jeb is actually stupid. He is too accomplished to be seriously stupid. Probably he is, like his brother George W. Bush, in the top decile of smarts. But, also like his brother, he comes off as lazy-minded and unimaginative, satisfied that he has mastered a topic once he's memorized a collection of clichés about it.

Certainly the clichés come thick and fast in *Immigration Wars*:

- Living "in the shadows"? Check!
- "Comprehensive reform"? Check!
- "Guest-worker program"? Check!
- "Broken system"? Check!
- Green cards for STEM graduates? Check!

Emma Lazarus is unaccountably left out. But no doubt that was an oversight.

I can't believe, either, that Jeb Bush is driven by conscious guile. With the Bushes, what you see is what you get. These are no Clintons or Nixons. Whereas Hillary Clinton always brings to my mind Dr. Johnson's remark about Alexander Pope ("He could not drink tea without a stratagem"), I can't imagine having such a thought about any Bush. They are transparently, sociopathically, self-interested.

A few years ago Steve Sailer came up with a sort of Kevin MacDonald-ish theory of the Bush clan: they were practicing a "group evolutionary strategy," optimizing their collective fitness at the expense of everyone around them—including, of course, the historic American nation.

Given that the Bush clan embraces a network of kith, kin, and business associations on both sides of the U.S.-Mexico border (Jeb's wife is Mexican-born and the family has many odd connections with the filthy-rich Mexican oligarchs), I'll allow that the theory has potential explanatory power. But I don't think we need to make recourse to biology here.

Most likely Jeb Bush is writing in a natural, effortless way for his fellow Tutsis, his fellow members of the Overclass. That he despises us Hutus is of no importance: so do the other Tutsis. Funneling candidates through the presidential primary process is now an entirely Tutsi operation, with Hutus allowed to participate only as light relief. This is a book for the funnelers.

Fortifying that explanation is the fact that *Immigration Wars* incorporates not merely one but *two* key components of Tutsi ideology: not just immigration romanticism but educational romanticism, too. (Over-educated themselves, the Tutsi aristocracy sees education as a balm for all wounds.)

In fact, we get a whole chapter titled "Immigration and Education."

The two romanticisms don't sit well together. If

Highly skilled immigrants take positions for which inadequate numbers of Americans are qualified [947]

Then, once we have fixed the education system as Jeb Bush proposes, why would we need skilled immigrants?

Later:

We would not need nearly so many immigrants if we were able to produce more highly skilled American students, workers, and creators. [1880]

But then wouldn't we lose all that "energy, vitality, talent, and enterprise" that is supposedly roaring in through the dam?

Jeb's not going to let a little contradiction like that slow him down. In the very next sentence he heads off into

> a second education challenge: the failure of our education system to provide high-quality opportunities for immigrant schoolchildren. [1881]

But why impose these unnecessary challenges on ourselves? As I noted satirically in my 2009 book *We Are Doomed*:

> If challenges are so good for us, why not create a few more? I suggest flooding some low-lying cities; causing landslides on inhabited hillsides with well-placed explosive charges; letting loose a few dangerous pathogens…. Or why not set off a nuclear weapon or two in populated areas to see how well we meet the challenge of swamped hospitals and mass evacuation? (p. 29)

And here, too, Jeb Bush is either telling careless lies, or else has not kept up with developments. He says:

> Florida's [accountability system] holds each student to the same high standard of achievement. It does not focus on a student's ethnic background or socioeconomic status. [1920]

Does it not? From the South Florida *Sun-Sentinel*, October 11, 2012:

> Florida's public school students will be judged in part by race and ethnicity, under new education benchmarks approved this week…. According to the plan, by 2018, the state wants 90 percent of Asian students, 88 percent of white, 81 percent of Hispanics and 74 percent of blacks to be at or above reading grade level.

Here too the clichés come thick and fast: charter schools, KIPP, online learning, accountability....

As with Emma Lazarus, we are at least spared Head Start.

The word "vocational" occurs nowhere in this book.

On the stopped-clock principle, Jeb Bush does get a couple of things right. He is rightly critical of chain migration and supportive of E-Verify.

It was nice, too, to see a *VDARE.com* article ("The Myth of the Hispanic Republicans," Sam Francis, January 23, 2003) quoted in the text and referenced in the end-notes. (His argument is not seriously addressed). But it would have been even nicer had Jeb Bush (or Clint Bolick, or their researcher) not mentioned Sam Francis in the present tense—apparently unaware that poor Sam left this world eight years ago.

Bush also takes a feeble stand against the "path to citizenship" for illegal aliens.

> A grant of citizenship is an undeserving [*sic*] reward for con-
> duct that we cannot afford to encourage. [598]

So, Bush says, illegals should get permanent residence, which in most cases is all they want, but not citizenship, which is much more important to Democratic vote-farmers than it is to the crop.

That particular policy proposal turns out to have been ill-timed. *Immigration Wars* went to press a few days before the Senatorial Gang of Eight revealed their amnesty-with-citizenship plan. Finding himself to the right of GOP Wonder Boy Marco Rubio, Bush has this week been engaged in what my automobile's GPS gadget calls "re-calculating." But, especially given that Bush had earlier indicated that he favored the "path to citizenship," it's an embarrassing fiasco, causing talk show host Mark Levin to suggest Bush hadn't read his own book. (Contrary to my assumption above—although *VDARE.com* Editor Peter Brimelow, who has Washington D.C. experience, thinks Levin may be right).

These small qualifications aside, this is a book of passionate, gushing immigration romanticism:

> Immigrants…are absolutely necessary to our future prosperity. But perhaps more than anything else, immigrants are essential for reminding us how special our nation is, and how hard it is to maintain freedom. [1855]

Immigration, on the romantic view, is in any case governed by a sort of conservation law, independent of its "absolute necessity." There is a fixed, irresistible quantity of immigrants, determined by some cosmic principle, and if you don't let them in legally, they will come in illegally.

> The combination of amnesty and inadequate avenues for legal immigration [in the 1986 IRCA] exacerbated the problem of illegal immigration. [1460]

Attempts to seal the border are therefore futile:

> For instance, a goal of sealing the border is hopeless without creating an immigration pipeline that provides a viable alternative to illegal immigration. [288]

Oh yeah? Perhaps we could take up a collection to send Jeb Bush on a fact-finding trip to Japan—or Israel.

Jeb Bush has written (or at least signed) a shallow, dishonest and—in its malign intent towards his fellow-citizens, in some sense treasonous—book.

So, on present form, he will be the 2016 Presidential nominee of Conservatism Inc./The Stupid Party.

* * *

This article can be read online at http://www.vdare.com/articles/ john-derbyshire-concludes-jeb-bush-just-doesn-t-like-americans-very-much

On Rand Paul and Ann Coulter:
Lose Some, Win Some, the War Grinds On

March 22, 2013

"One in, one out," my mother was sometimes heard to remark after her regular evening perusal of the Northampton *Chronicle and Echo*. We knew, without needing to ask, that this was a reference to her favorite section of that newspaper, the "Births, Marriages, and Deaths" columns—the "Hatched, Matched, and Dispatched" in our household's micro-dialect. Her meaning was that some family we knew had been blessed with a new baby while some other family had suffered a bereavement.

This past week was a bit like that on the patriotic immigration front. We lost one big name, but gained another.

The "one out" was Rand Paul. Was he ever actually *in*, though? My colleagues think not. He had depressed me, too, with his response to the State of the Union speech in February.

Two and a half years before *that* I had actually asked Paul face-to-face for his thoughts on immigration. This was during his Senate run in 2010. He had dropped in to the *National Review* offices to give us face time, as candidates do. (See "Ten Things You Should Know about Rand Paul," Kevin D. Williamson, July 13, 2010, which doesn't mention immigration.)

I can't locate any video of the meeting, and all I can find in my notes is:

immigr: not much clue

…but I am a poor note-taker, so that can't be taken as dispositive as to Rand's 2010 immigration position.

Paul made his exit from the zone of immigration patriotism—or, if you prefer, made it indisputably clear that he had never really belonged in that zone—with a disgraceful speech to the U.S. Hispanic Chamber of Commerce on Tuesday.

For Senator Paul to speak at all to an organization whose name contains the word "Hispanic"—a bogus ethnicity concocted for political purposes by Nixon-era bureaucrats—was sufficiently regrettable.

But Paul compounded the offense by delivering part of his speech in Spanish. John Quincy Adams *refused on principle* to use his fluent German when courting German-speaking voters. However, "on principle" is not a phrase that leaps to mind when one surveys the present-day Republican Party. (With a few honorable exceptions.)

Nor does the actual content of Paul's speech bear very close inspection. One-third of the Spanish-language section was given over to a quotation from poet Pablo Neruda. Like Paul, Neruda served in his nation's Senate...but representing the Chilean Communist Party. Neruda's poetry may be first-rate for all I know, and it has often been remarked that politics makes strange bedfellows; but it seems odd for a libertarian to seek inspiration from a recipient of the Stalin Peace Prize.

The rest of Paul's speech is a drivel of clichés, drawn about equally from George W. Bush's fatuous "compassionate conservatism" ("we also must treat those [illegals] who are already here with understanding and compassion") and from the left-activist prompt book ("the struggle for a good education is the civil rights issue of our day"). (In regard to that latter, I note once again in passing the now-routine yoking of the two great soft-headed feel-good fantasies of our time: educational romanticism and immigration romanticism).

Of course, Paul's defection—clarification, whatever—is a blow to patriotic immigration reform. The man is a national legislator, a United States Senator. He is also an adornment of the Tea Party, which can fairly be credited with the GOP's 2010 triumph in the House of Representatives. Rand Paul is a serious congressional player, directly and indirectly. That the congressional Treason Lobby has acquired a new recruit is a major reverse for good sense on immigration.

Looking at wider trends, Paul's defection represents a triumph of globalist, nation-denying neolibertarianism over paleolibertarianism, defined by Arthur Pendleton on *VDARE.com* as "the once-promising intellectual movement that stayed true to libertarian principles while opposing Open Borders, libertinism, egalitarianism, and Political Correctness."

What made this happen? Did the money people get to Paul?

I have trouble believing this. Paul seemed to me, face to face, to be a decent person from the same mold as his father. It's hard to imagine either man selling out his principles for campaign cash...though I suppose the shade of Britain's notoriously cynical eighteenth-century Prime Minister Sir Robert ("All those men have their price") Walpole is chuckling somewhere out of sight.

In seeking an explanation, I am more inclined to impersonal historical forces. Reading Paul's speech, in fact, what came to mind— and I mean no disrespect to the dead—was that awful story out of Florida a few weeks ago, about the poor chap who was swallowed by a sinkhole while watching TV in bed.

Rand Paul suffered some analogous political fate. Playing the part of the Florida terrain here is the intellectual framework of our current politics: a thin crust of firm civic republicanism overlaying a deep wet karst of utopian romanticism. Playing the part of aquifer depletion is the draining away of national spirit under the forces of multiculturalism and ethnomasochism. Playing the part of gravity is the Republican Party's current, powerful death wish.

GLWOOP! There goes another one.

And, as always in human affairs, sheer stupidity and sloth are not to be neglected. Given that Rand Paul's speech was stitched together from the stalest, most threadbare clichés—the kind of thing immigration patriots have been debunking for a decade and more—you have to wonder how much time the junior Senator from Kentucky put into reading up on his chosen topic.

Indeed, you have to wonder the same thing about most of the people in public life who make policy on, or even just pontificate about, immigration. I should be very surprised to learn that more than half our national legislators know the difference between immigrant and nonimmigrant visas; or that more than a tenth of them could distinguish an H-1B from an H-2A.

Policy wonkery can sometimes be annoying, it's true. But on the whole knowledge is good, especially when one is debating critical national policies.

For example, it could have saved Paul from today's further embarrassment:

> Sen. Rand Paul said Thursday that the nation's current immigration policies are "de facto amnesty," hitting back against his conservative critics—including Ann Coulter and Rush Limbaugh—who say he's supporting amnesty for illegal immigrants. ["Rand Paul: 'De facto Amnesty' Already Here," Kevin Cirilli, *Politico*, March 21, 2013.]

Paul apparently thinks (or has been told) that this is an original and compelling argument. But in fact, of course, it has long been debunked and discredited.

We peg away at explaining, exposing, chronicling, and documenting; yet somehow none of it, not a word, reaches the aery heights in which dwell our political masters. They run on fumes: fumes from half-baked, half-remembered sophistries they read somewhere or heard from a lobbyist, and from faddish pseudo-emotions barely reflected upon. Data? Who needs data?

So much for the "one out." The "one in" was Ann Coulter, who told CPAC last Saturday afternoon:

> I'm now a single-issue voter against amnesty…. We offer hope, opportunity, and jobs. And I *hope* that we offer a change to our absolutely suicidal immigration policies.

Ann is not a legislator, although I understand that Peter Brimelow is having some COULTER FOR PRESIDENT lapel buttons made up. She is a brilliant and popular polemicist, though, and her speech—and the applause it got from the CPAC crowd—could be a milestone on the road back from the demoralized GOP's surrender on immigration.

It is good to know, too, that the lady has decisively unhitched herself from the gun-controlling, border-opening Chris Christie. Ann signaled her refusal to be embarrassed about that error by opening her CPAC talk with a Christie joke: "The sequester's really ruined everything, hasn't it?... Even CPAC had to cut back on its speakers this year by about 300 pounds." (At 20 seconds in, http://youtu.be/9KSsep00x6M?t=19s)

The *chutzpah* is characteristic, and welcome in a movement that has all too often in recent years been timidly deferential to the established liberal order.

Ann does not embarrass easy. When *National Review* dropped her from its contributor columns in October 2001 for urging missionary wars against terrorist nations, she famously described its editors as "girly-boys" and scoffed:

> "If *National Review* has no spine, they are not my allies. I really don't need friends like that. Every once in a while they'll throw one of their people to the wolves to get good press in left-wing publications." ["*National Review* Fires Ann Coulter," Anthony York, *Salon.com*, October 2, 2001.]

Just so.

I want to hear what Ann has to say about *legal* immigration— about the lottery, chain migration, the "refugee" and "skilled worker" rackets—before I buy one of those lapel buttons. But I welcome her into the stockade.

And I wish her all the luck in the world at surviving what will now be thrown at her by the forces of Conservatism, Inc.

So: one out, one in. You win some, you lose some. The war grinds on.

* * *

This article can be read online at http://www.vdare.com/articles/
john-derbyshire-on-rand-paul-and-ann-coulter-lose-some-win-some-
the-war-grinds-on

If There Is Hope, It Lies in the Comment Threads

May 16, 2013

(With apologies to George Orwell)

As depressing as most of the blogging on the Jason Richwine affair has been, the comment threads have been more so. Discussions of race, of IQ, and, by some kind of multiplicative principle, even more so of race-and-IQ tap into a deep vein of willful ignorance and moralistic posturing.

Godwin's Law applies of course; but we really need a whole sheaf of such laws for these comment threads. Merely as an example, I hereby propose Derbyshire's Law Of Race And/Or IQ Comment Threads:

> **Derbyshire's Law**: As the comment thread following an online article relating to race and/or IQ grows longer, the probability of a commenter declaring that Stephen Jay Gould's book *The Mismeasure of Man* is the last word on the subject approaches 1.

In this *Gawker.com* thread ["A Reader's Guide to Andrew Sullivan's Defense of Race Science," Max Read, November 29, 2011], for example, the third commenter (out of 123 at the time of writing) is a Gould groupie—apparently unaware, as are the rest of them, that Gould is now dispositively known to have cooked at least some of his data. ["Study Debunks Stephen Jay Gould's Claim of Racism on Morton Skulls," Nicholas Wade, *New York Times*, June 13, 2011.]

Similar laws govern the inevitability of appearance by other pet race-and-IQ-denialist talking points: Henry Goddard's 1913 studies of immigrants (perhaps *VDARE.com* should organize some kind of centenary celebration?), Lewontin's Fallacy, epigenetics, cultural bias in tests, poverty-not-race, zzzzzzz....

62

On the glass-half-full side, there are an encouraging number of *informed* comments scattered among the dross. Even at frankly Leninist websites like *Daily Kos*, the comment threads contain contributions like these.[1] (Reading through that site I notice yet again the great fondness Leftists have for dirty words. The heritage here goes back beyond Lenin to Marx himself.)

So it hasn't been all depressing. In fact, there may in these comment threads be a counter to the despair one often hears from Dissident Right figures.

At last month's American Renaissance conference, for example, Jared Taylor said that when he'd started the group 23 years ago, he'd assumed he would gradually be able to get race-realist ideas out into the public forum for reasoned discussion.

And yet, said Jared, such discussion is more difficult now than ever, as the shutting-down of AmRen's conferences in 2010 and 2011 showed. I think the Jason Richwine business also illustrates Jared's point. Hence the note of despair. (I hear it in Pat Buchanan's recent writings, too.)

Why this narrowing of the zone of permissible debate? Well, an entirely new generation has been born and come to adulthood since 1990, while at the same time the last generation that matured before the Great Disruption of the 1960s has retired from key positions in law, education, and the media.

Thus the working population of the U.S.A. is now composed of people who grew up being expected, by those who instructed and entertained them, to internalize the feel-good utopian-egalitarian fantasies about human nature that dominated the late-20th-century West—Cultural Marxism.

---

[1] http://www.dailykos.com/comments/1207817/50127117#c16 and http://www.dailykos.com/comments/1207817/50136695#c327

That some fair portion of these later generations resisted the relentless propaganda is a tribute to human orneriness. And that portion has survived, with their reasoning faculties intact, into an era of deepening understanding in the human sciences.

For we now know more than we did 23 years ago. Of the 176 references I counted at the end of Jason Richwine's dissertation, 132—precisely three-quarters—are from later than 1990. The longest chapter in *The Mismeasure of Man*, by contrast, is devoted to a fanatically detailed (but debatable) debunking of Cyril Burt, who retired from academic work in 1951.

Hence the push-back you see against Cultural Marxism in these comment threads—although since these are essentially scientific topics, "Cultural Lysenkoism" might be a more apt term.

If there are grains of hope to be found in the Jason Richwine comment threads, there are great boulders of the stuff in comment threads on the Rubio-Schumer immigration bill. Conservatism, Inc. may be Open Borders enthusiasts in obedience to their big donors, but people who post comments on conservative websites want none of it. Here are the first four comments on a random immigration story at a conservative website:

- No more 1986 amnesty. It was a failure then, it will be a failure now....

- We don't need any new laws. Just secure the border and enforce current immigration laws....

- All the points made by so many of the citizens on this blog are correct when it comes to the Senate's GROSS BETRAYAL OF AMERICANS....

- Anything short of a mass exodus of illegals and a really tall wall at the border isn't gonna do....

["Crumbling Coalition? First Cracks in Immigration Deal Emerge," Stephen Dinan, *Washington Times*, May 12, 2013.]

Nor is it only at conservative outlets that the comment threads lean to immigration patriotism. Try this news story: "1 in 3 Adults in Parts of L.A. Are in U.S. Illegally, Study Finds," Cindy Chang, *Los Angeles Times*, May 8, 2013. Or this opinion column: "Immigration Exclusionists Out of Touch," Jennifer Rubin, *Washington Post*, April 25, 2013. Or this left-liberal website: "Deportation Without Representation: Immigrants Who Are Detained Should Have a Right to a Lawyer," Mark Noferi, *Slate.com*, May 15, 2013.

Sometimes at liberal outlets the skepticism comes from the Left, as with the comment thread to this *New York Times* story. Sample comments:

- This should cause even the most liberal among us to pause giving their support to this bill. If so many wealthy people want this it can`t be good for the rest of us....

- Corporate profits do not outweigh the health of the U.S. and the proper employment of U.S. citizens....

- Instead of listening to well qualified but unemployed U.S. workers the politicians are listening to billionaires who could care less about the U.S. workers....

["Latest Product From Tech Firms: An Immigration Bill," Eric Lipton and Somini Sengupta, May 4, 2013.]

All very hopeful. How seriously should we take comment threads, though? Do they in any degree represent the voice of the people? Or are they only the voices of cranks, neurotics, and monomaniacs?

Or something even worse than that, perhaps. In communist China it has for years been an open secret that the Party recruits legions of college students to post blogs, comments, Amazon reviews, and the like giving the Party's line on issues of the day. The going rate is 50

Chinese cents—*wu mao* in Chinese—per posting. The commenters are known in aggregate as the *Wu Mao Dang*, the Fifty Cent Party.

I am told the Israeli government does something similar. If so, that means that other nations keen to influence public discussions in directions favorable to themselves—the Saudis, the Russians—are also in the game.

It doesn't seem very likely that the Chinese or Israeli game would include immigration-patriotic postings on U.S. websites, but who knows?

Even assuming that commenters are human beings of normal psychology and not in anyone's pay, can they be taken as representative of a readership? It seems intuitive that some sort of power law is in play: a handful of compulsive commentators contributing hundreds of comments per week, a larger number of merely-keen commenters contributing dozens each, then a much larger number of the not-easily-stirred sending in the occasional one or two comments.

(Our own Steve Sailer is hovering on the edge of compulsivity, at least in regard to topics that particularly interest him. A few days ago a friend emailed me with: "Go to here and type Ctrl-F 'sailer'...." I did so. Steve had contributed *fifty-four comments* to a single blog post at *Marginal Revolution*. ["Which Athletes and Entertainers Choose to Come Out of the Closet?" Tyler Cowen, May 6, 2013.] How does he find the *time?* And suffer so many fools so gladly?)

There are other considerations to weigh when judging the usefulness of comment threads as a guide to opinion: the vexed question of thread moderation, for example.

There is, in fact, probably a Ph.D. dissertation to be written on comment threads. Probably some sociology major is already at work on one. What kind of thing might he come up with?

To try to get some kind of a handle on this, a few days ago I ran a quick'n'dirty analysis of the comment thread to an opinion column on the immigration topic. For comparison I then did the same analysis for a different, but equally controversial topic from the same columnist. As this comparison topic I chose gun control.

For my columnist to be analyzed I wanted a straight-ticket, check-all-boxes, unimaginative, both-knees-jerking-in-unison Left-liberal. I settled on Eleanor Clift.

Ms. Clift posts articles at *Daily Beast*. Her April 25th column praised the co-operation between Senators McCain and Schumer on the immigration bill, which she takes for granted is a Good Thing with widespread public support:

> Polls show that 70 percent of the American people favor immigration reform, and a poll released Thursday taken by Americans for Tax Reform found two-thirds of Republicans support the Senate bill as it's been described. ["Gloves Off on Immigration Bill as McCain, Schumer Go to the Mat," *Daily Beast*, April 25, 2013.]

At the time I checked there were 21 *original* comments—i.e. not counting replies to comments, replies to replies, and so on, which tend to wander away in off-topic directions, mainly directions of petty bickering and personal vituperation.

The 21 broke 6-15 for-against Ms. Clift. To put it differently, original commenters were 2.5 to 1 against the lady. Call that the "hostility ratio."

Those 21 comments came from 17 persons, or at any rate handles. One person might, of course, have several handles; but since I have no way to investigate this, I'll assume that one handle is one person. Let's call this a "persistence ratio"—the persistence, that is, of particular persons in posting more than one original comment—of 21 to 17, or 1.24.

For comparison, let's consider Ms. Clift's column on gun control ["Joe Manchin's Crusade to Get Gun Bill a Second Shot," *Daily Beast*, May 1, 2013].

At the time I checked, half an hour after the previous analysis, there were 151 original comments posted from 121 persons, breaking 69-82 for-against the author. That's a hostility ratio of 1.2, a persistence ratio of 1.25.

From this very sketchy analysis I shall boldly draw the following conclusions:

- Ms. Clift's Beltway-wonkish opinion on the prospects for federal gun-control legislation was unpopular with her readers, but....

- Her left-utopian position on immigration was *twice* as unpopular.

- The persistence ratio was essentially identical for the two columns, with ninety percent of readers contributing just one or two comments each.

In case you're wondering, the Godwin Quotient—percentage length into the comment thread at which one of the words "Nazi" or "Hitler" appears—was 0.43 for the gun-control column, zero for the shorter immigration piece.

However, as you will know if you clicked on the links for either of those two columns, *Daily Beast* no longer shows comments. This is a development of just the past few days; I gathered my numbers on May 8th.

That is probably the most significant thing of all. It's a chore to maintain and moderate comment blogs. (*VDARE.com*, as we have to keep explaining, simply doesn't have the resources.) If Eleanor Clift's comment threads are typical, for leftist web sites with those high hostility ratios it is a *dispiriting* chore.

It is therefore a pretty safe prediction that more and more websites will, like *Daily Beast*, shut down comments. They will excuse themselves by arguing that the same discussions can take place on social media like Twitter or on internet communities like *Reddit* and *Slash-dot*.

Perhaps that's right. Not having a clue how any of those things work, I can't pass judgment.

My advice to the guy doing his Ph.D. dissertation on comment threads: get a move on and get the darn thing approved before everyone's forgotten what a comment thread is.

* * *

This article can be read online at http://www.vdare.com/articles/john-derbyshire-says-if-there-is-hope-it-lies-in-the-comment-threads

Do We Need More Smart Foreigners?

May 23, 2013

In all the fuss over Jason Richwine's Ph.D. dissertation, "IQ and Immigration," there has been surprisingly little commentary on the main idea of the thing, *viz.* that, to quote the author (p. 133):

> I believe there is a strong case for IQ selection [of immigrants], since it is theoretically a win-win for the U.S. and for potential immigrants.

Let's discard the last four words there for starters. The welfare of foreigners is no proper concern of U.S. policy-makers. I was a foreigner myself until age 56. It never occurred to me that the U.S.A. should expend a single dollar or bead of sweat on behalf of my well-being, except to enhance its own.

What about the rest, the proposition that IQ selection of immigrants is a win for the U.S.A.? Jason Richwine is, of course, not the only one to have said so. Recall Mitt Romney in last year's election, vowing to staple a Green Card to the graduation diplomas of foreign STEM students.

It sounds like a good idea—wouldn't it be great to have more smart people!—but there are a number of problems with it.

In the first place, we must beware of the Linear Fallacy. That's the argument that if one of something is good, then two must be twice as good, and ten must be ten times as good.

Practically nothing works like that. I'll allow a handful of exceptions—number of dollars in one's bank balance, for example—but in most things the law of diminishing returns holds sway, and the linear principle delivers results that are unpleasant (salt in the stew) or even fatal (medication dosage).

Very few graphs are straight lines. Very few even consistently head in one direction, up or down. It's a nonlinear world.

How many smart people does a society need for stability and prosperity? This is not a question that has received as much attention as, it seems to me, it ought.

Some years ago the anonymous statistician "La Griffe du Lion" (readers of *Unknown Quantity* will get the reference) came up with Smart Fraction Theory (SFT):

> For a technologically sophisticated society, SFT asserts that a nation's per capita GDP is determined by the population fraction with IQ greater than or equal to some threshold IQ. Consistent with the data of Lynn and Vanhanen, that threshold IQ is 108, a bit less than the minimum required for what used to be a bachelor's degree.

In other words, La Griffe is saying that if X is the proportion of your population with IQ greater than 108, then there is a lower bound for X, below which your country, in the absence of exceptional natural resources, cannot be prosperous and stable.

(On a normal "bell curve" distribution, the actual percentage value of X for populations with mean IQ 80, 85, 90, 95, 100, 105, 110, 115 would be, to the nearest percent: 3, 6, 12, 19, 30, 42, 55, 68, respectively. So the Netherlands, with mean IQ 100, has a 30 percent smart fraction, while Japan, at 105, has 42 percent, and Turkey, at 90, has only 12 percent.)

La Griffe hints at, but does not discuss, the idea that as well as a lower bound for X, there may also be an *upper* bound. That is, it may be the case that it is bad for a country to have *too many* smart people.

If you have mixed with many classes and races of people, your experience will suggest this. A certain unimaginative, not-very-reflective, commonsensical approach to life, shared by many citizens, provides valuable ballast, keeping society on an even keel.

William F. Buckley's famous observation that "I should sooner live in a society governed by the first two thousand names in the Boston telephone directory than in a society governed by the two thousand faculty members of Harvard University" [*Rumbles Left and Right*, 1963, p. 134] was surely well-founded.

If that is right, then too much of a reduction in the quantity of that ballast would be socially destabilizing. A too-high value of X would have just that effect.

There are other considerations, too. There may, for instance, be biological downsides to smartness.

There certainly seem to be in the case of Ashkenazi-Jewish smarts. The 2006 paper on this subject from the University of Utah argued plausibly that the strong pressure of natural selection increased medieval Ashkenazi intelligence to the sensational modern mean IQ of 112-115; but that it also increased the frequency of nervous-system genetic disorders. Population-genetic changes are often a matter of swings and roundabouts, of two steps forward and one step back.

Even without that intensive overclocking, there may be unavoidable biological downsides to high IQ.

East Asians (China, Korea, Japan) have mean IQ of 106. That's nothing like as high as the Ashkenazi mean, but it may come with some similar side effects. In international comparisons of personality traits, East Asians score highest on neuroticism: see for example Figure 4 on page 201 in "The Geographic Distribution of Big Five Personality Traits," http://biculturalism.ucr.edu/pdfs/Schmitt%20et%20al_JCCP2007.pdf.

This agrees with anecdotal observations. If you live much among East Asians you notice that an unusual proportion of them are slightly nutty, though mostly in a quiet, harmless way.

> One of the maddest things about Japan is that Japanese madmen do not get mad…. The prototype of the Japanese madman is the gentle, docile, withdrawn, well-behaved mental patient. Violent emotional display is simply 'not done,' even among lunatics. [*The Lotus and the Robot*, by Arthur Koestler, p. 201.]

So it may be that the current Chinese drive to raise national IQ via eugenics ought to come with a warning label: BE CAREFUL WHAT YOU WISH FOR.

And then there is the matter of social frictions.

When not thinking very hard, we Americans tend to suppose that friction between races is driven by notions of *superiority*—of the more intelligent and industrious race looking down on the duller and lazier. That is what Americans generally mean when they speak of "racism." It has obvious roots in the U.S.A.'s own racial history.

Yet in fact most of the world's racial resentments have been aimed in the opposite direction: *against the more clever and industrious*. Jews weren't persecuted for all those centuries because people thought they were dumb or lazy.

Traditional American race prejudice was aimed both down *and* up. Blacks were believed to be stupid and lazy, so that they would end up being a burden on the white population.

Where East Asians had settled on the West Coast, however, the prejudice was that they were *too* clever and industrious, so that whites would end up working under them—an indignity not to be borne:

> Representative MacLafferty emphasized Japanese domination of certain agricultural markets (*Cong. Rec.*, April 5, 1924, p. 5681), and Representative Lea noted their ability to supplant "their American competitor" (*Cong. Rec.*, April 5, 1924, p. 5697). Representative Miller described the Japanese as "a relentless and unconquerable competitor of our people wherever he places himself" (*Cong. Rec.*, April 8, 1924, p. 5884)....
> [*The Culture of Critique,* Kevin MacDonald, 1998 edition, p. 268.]

These complementary prejudices were sometimes combined in a Goldilocks thesis: the black race was too dumb to achieve anything, the yellow race was too smart for its own good, but Europeans had just the right balance of intelligence and stolid good sense.

I don't think it's a stretch to say that History is not altogether un-friendly to this thesis. Still, you don't need race differences to favor the middle way on intelligence.

> In a now famous speech delivered in March 1991...[Serb leader Slobodan] Milosevic declared to thunderous applause: "If we must fight, then my God we will fight. And I hope they [i.e. the other populations of disintegrating Yugoslavia] will not be so crazy as to fight against us. Because *if we don't know how to work well or to do business,* at least we know how to fight well!" [*World on Fire,* Amy Chua, p. 174, her italics.]

Everyday notions of prejudice revolve around arrogant majorities convinced of their own innate superiority beating up on helpless mi-norities.

This is a false picture. In fact a real conviction of one's group's superiority at least as often leads to pity and paternalism. Aggressive group violence is usually directed at those who "know how to work well or do business."

One way or another, then, it may be that the Richwine-Romney idea of improving your nation by importing smart foreigners is wrong-headed.

We surely don't need any more dumb people in the U.S.A. than we already have. That we need more smart people is, however, open to reasonable doubt.

* * *

This article can be read online at http://www.vdare.com/articles/ john-derbyshire-asks-do-we-need-more-smart-foreigners

Guess What?—Schumer-Rubio Ignores Collision Course Between Affirmative Action and Immigration

June 6, 2013

The Schumer-Rubio Amnesty/Immigration Surge Bill emerged from the Senate Judiciary committee May 21st. The full Senate will consider a motion to vote on the bill (after having first, of course, pondered a motion to vote on the motion to vote) next Monday, June 10th.

So far as I can ascertain, neither the bill nor the 161 amendments the committee considered contained the phrase "Affirmative Action." This is a pity, as the intersection of these two issues—immigration and Affirmative Action—is a place where current social policy shows itself at its most flagrantly illogical.

For immigration patriots, Affirmative Action is a good point of leverage: unpopular in itself, and doubly outrageous as affected by immigration. Affirmative Action is a zero-sum game, and allowing immigrants to benefit from it while simultaneously increasing their numbers inevitably dispossesses white Americans even faster. This issue was raised by the historian Hugh Graham, in *Collision Course*, as long ago as 2002.

With a Supreme Court decision on the Fisher case due any time now, coinciding with the Gang of Eight bill, that zone of intersection between the two issues is in the spotlight. This is a good time to brush up on Affirmative Action.

Probably most Americans who accept Affirmative Action assume that it still has its original purpose: to compensate American blacks for their ancestors' status as slaves or second-class citizens. Yet:

> Blacks of West Indian or African parentage are greatly over-represented at the more competitive colleges compared to all blacks. At the Ivy League schools represented in the NLSF survey blacks with parents born abroad—mostly those from

75

West Indian and African backgrounds—constitute 40 percent of all black students, an enormous overrepresentation considering the small percentage (approximately 13 percent) such students represent in the total black student age population in America.... Immigrant-origin blacks compete with native-origin blacks for affirmative-action slots in elite universities, a development some native blacks find objectionable. (p. 280)

That is from Russell Nieli's recent book *Wounds That Will Not Heal: Affirmative Action and Our Continuing Racial Divide* (New York: Encounter Books, 2012).

Nieli, who teaches politics at Princeton University, lays into his subject with gusto, declaring in his introduction that

40+ years of racial preference policies [have] had overwhelmingly negative consequences.... Affirmative Action has been a disaster on multiple levels.

Nieli works his way painstakingly through all those levels, though concentrating almost exclusively on college admissions. Quotes here are from his book.

- *Affirmative Action fortifies prejudice:*

Affirmative-action role models are not genuine and are soon recognized as such by all concerned. The role actually modeled by Affirmative Action recipients is that of a patronized black, Hispanic, or female who is of inferior qualifications...and who would not have gotten to where he or she is except for the existence of an official policy of government favoritism....

Resentments inevitably abound, especially among white and Asian students who remember disappointed high school friends and rejected applicants of their own race, some of whom were much better qualified than many of the black and Hispanic students they meet on campus.

(Resentments of that kind, while surely easy for most people to understand, have baffled at least one Supreme Court Justice.)

- *Affirmative Action, with its associated rewards and resentments, strengthens ethnic tribalism,* which "is a principle of social chaos and, ultimately, a formula for civil war."

- *Fundamental American norms of fairness and reciprocity are violated by Affirmative Action:*

  White people, even very bigoted ones, can accept the advancement of blacks, or of any other racial, ethnic, or religious group in America, within virtually any area of endeavor, so long as that advancement takes place within the accepted rules of the game.

Which is to say, within those fundamental norms of fairness and reciprocity.

- *The "pipeline problem":*

  NAM (black and Hispanic) students exhibiting low average performance at all levels of the educational system—is made worse by Affirmative Action in college admissions.

  NAM students admitted on lower standards than whites and Asians will *of course* underperform in their college careers.

- *The related "mismatch problem":*

  The subject of *Mismatch: How Affirmative Action Hurts Students It's Intended to Help, and Why Universities Won't Admit It,* this problem arises when NAM students who might prosper and develop confidence in lower-ranked colleges flounder in elite schools, while those low-ranked colleges are deprived of students who might add luster to their reputations.

(Russell Nieli told me that if you read *Mismatch* and his book, you will have the complete case against Affirmative Action in detail. I am sure he's right; but both are scholarly books written in measured tones. If your taste runs to something with more polemical zip, I recommend Steven Farron's 2005 book *The Affirmative Action Hoax.*)

The lower-ranked colleges respond by "downward-raiding," admitting NAM students who would be happier and more successful at still less competitive schools…and so on downwards, mismatching at all levels.

- ### *Disincentives:*

Knowing that their race or ethnicity will waft them into a good college, smart NAM high-school students "will have every reason to work less and devote more time to fun-producing activities."

- ### *Dishonesty:*

The rationale for Affirmative Action has seen a flagrant moving of the goalposts.

Affirmative Action began in the 1960s as a scheme of compensatory justice, with an additional basis in the "social need" for more black professionals.

When Affirmative Action came before the Supreme Court in the 1978 *Bakke* case, however, these foundations were found to be at odds with the 14th Amendment's guarantee of equal treatment. So the supposed benefits of "diversity" were hastily drafted in as a substitute rationale—a "compelling state interest"—for continuing race preferences.

Suddenly the argument from compensatory justice was no longer much heard, just as "before [the Court's] decision, diversity-enhancement arguments were rare to non-existent."

- *The discredited "Contact Hypothesis":*

The notion that diversity is beneficial in and by itself is based on the "Contact Hypothesis" theory which states that: "Prejudice of a racial or ethnic kind and the negative stereotyping that promotes it are products of social isolation and ignorance of the 'other' that such isolation produces.... Better contact furthers better understanding."

Nieli shows that the Contact Hypothesis is now known, as dispositively as anything *can* be known in the social sciences, to be false.

Wounds That Will Not Heal is anchored at two points of general philosophy.

Underlying his outlook, Nieli tells us, is Personalism, the individualistic creed sired by liberal-Jeffersonian "rights" doctrine out of Christianity.

> The early and mid-1960s marked a high point in post-Reconstruction American history in the public understanding of, and respect for, the dignity and worth of individual human persons.

But:

> The period from the very late 1960s and early 1970s proved to be a period of unprecedented ethnicization and tribalization in the American public consciousness.

Nieli favors the earlier dispensation.

The second anchor point, unusually for books from social-science academics, is a respectful attitude to evolutionary psychology.

If you are one of those who know your way around this stretch of savannah, you will find, while reading *Wounds That Will Not Heal*, that you keep coming across terms, references, and names that are familiar. The Environment of Evolutionary Adaptedness, for example, gets a friendly mention.

E.O. Wilson isn't referenced, but at least James Q. Wilson (*Crime & Human Nature* with Richard Herrnstein) is. So is Lawrence Keeley (*War Before Civilization*). So—good grief!—is J. Philippe Rushton (*Race, Evolution & Behavior*), of whom:

> Some find Rushton's ideas incendiary, although like any theory in social science they must be validated or refuted based on the best evidence, not the most widely shared ideology.

Fat chance!...but a rare breath of calm good sense none the less.

Nieli does not go all the way to Frank Salter's arguments about social bonding based on genetic interests. He restricts himself to culturalist "blank slate" explanations for group differences. But in the milieu in which he wants to present his arguments, this is as far as you can go without being Watsoned.

When dealing with the generality of social scientists, it's a stretch even to get them to culturalism. Their preferred mode of thinking about negative group characteristics, Nieli tells us, is in terms of outside agency. NAMs have low test scores, high crime rates, lots of fatherlessness? Oh, that's all caused by white racism, you know.

> In my own experience I have found that the only way to get left-oriented sociologists to acknowledge the possible salience of cultural factors in explaining the poor academic performance of so many black and Latino youth is to bring up the alternative explanation of genes. 'So if it isn't culture, do you think the problem is related to genes?'... Instantly under such prodding leftist sociologists become born-again culturalists and eagerly embrace the theories of people like John Ogbu and Thomas Sowell, whom they normally would ignore or spend considerable effort trying to refute.

I'm not sure how much this approach helps. Isn't anything *prior* to culture? What are the upstream variables? Where should we go looking for them? "In white racism, in historical injustice," that leftist sociologist would presumably reply. "In feedback loops of population genetics and historical experience," I would say.

What would Russell Nieli say? I think he'd say that he has an open mind on the matter, and will be content to have contributed somehow to discrediting the hideous, dishonest, divisive racket of Affirmative Action.

It's a solid and honorable position. In the present constrained atmosphere in which these topics are discussed, it's even quite a brave one for an academic to take.

Russell Nieli has written a useful, important, and timely book. I wish him well with it.

* * *

This article can be read online at http://www.vdare.com/articles/ guess-what-schumer-rubio-ignores-collision-course-between- affirmative-action-and-immigratio

Demographic Disasters—China's and Ours

June 13, 2013

One can never have enough lessons in humility. A month or so after publishing a book titled *From the Dissident Right*, last weekend I found myself among some *real* dissidents.

This was the dinner for Professor Zhang Yitang I mentioned in "Off-Topic: An Exciting Invitation to Meet a Mathematician," *VDare.com*, May 27, 2013. Prof. Zhang is currently famous for having cracked an outstanding mathematical problem earlier this year. ["Solving a Riddle of Primes," Kenneth Chang, *NYT,* May 20, 2013.] The dinner was organized by old friends of his—mainland Chinese who had, like him, come to study in the U.S.A. in the 1980s. Most of them had had some association with the Chinese Alliance for Democracy, which flourished in the 1980s and 1990s among expatriate Chinese intellectuals.

It was humbling to be among these people. One fellow diner had spent eleven years in jail, much of it in solitary confinement. Another had been imprisoned for four years *at the age of sixteen* after participating in the 1978-79 "Democracy Wall" movement. (She now works for a New York-registered foundation, Women's Rights In China.)

The word "dissident" may be etymologically correct for those of us Americans who sit apart when the community singing is going on, but it seems a tad impertinent in company like this.

Although the general mood was one of celebration for Prof. Zhang's achievement, there was a whiff of melancholy about the occasion. The democracy movement's U.S. branch has quiesced; their magazine has suspended publication; the activists have built lives and careers for themselves here in the U.S.A. and drifted away from each other.

One of them remarked to me wistfully at the dinner that it had been many years since she'd seen so many of that generation of dissidents all together in one place.

It didn't help that last week marked the 24th anniversary of the Chinese government's crushing of the student movement in Tiananmen Square. Twenty-four may not seem like a very round number to Westerners, but it is precisely two duodecadal cycles of the traditional Chinese calendar: 1989 and 2013 are both Years of the Snake. My dinner partners had it in mind.

In the context of U.S. politics, this was also the week when China's new leader Xi Jinping paid a call on Barack Obama, while Chinese blogs had just got through batting around some controversial remarks Joe Biden made at a commencement speech last month. (The remarks went unnoticed here—who pays attention to anything Joe Biden says?—but caused a stir over there.)

It has therefore been with China on my mind that I've been watching the SchMcGRubio Amnesty/Immigration Surge bill drag its weary length along through the U.S. Senate chamber.

For better or worse, our two nations look set to dominate geopolitics across the next few years, yoked together in a to-and-fro dance of mutual dependency and mutual suspicion.

Some problems we have that they don't, mainly our vast and unsustainable public debt. Some they have that we don't: massive environmental degradation, restless border colonies. We also have some problems in common: slowing economies, unemployed college graduates, widening wealth gaps.

(Class resentment in China when I lived there 30 years ago was aimed at the *gao-gan-zi-di*—the "princeling" offspring of senior Party officials and old revolutionaries. Nowadays there is a whole menagerie of spoiled brats: *fu-er-dai, guan-er-dai, xing-er-dai, hong-er-dai*…I find it hard to remember which is which. There's a taxonomy at http://www.tealeafnation.com/2013/03/born-rich-in-china-explaining-the-disdain-for-fuerdai).

And then, in the longer term, there are the prospects of demographic disaster, for them and for us.

For us, continued mass non-European immigration will reduce the nation's founding stock to a minority by mid-century. We shall then be a majority-minority nation. The history of such nations, except under strong imperial-authoritarian control, is not encouraging.

For China, the possibility of demographic disaster arises from decades of low fertility and the associated issue of skewed sex ratios. China's one-child policy is usually fingered as the main culprit, but given the similar demographic histories of post-WW2 Japan, South Korea, and Taiwan, I doubt the policy has been anything more than an accelerant.

The key statistic here is Total Fertility Rate (TFR): the number of children a woman would expect to have in her fertile years if, at every age, she duplicated today's rate for that age. Given zero net immigration, a TFR of 2.1 means stable population numbers. The U.S.A., with current TFR 2.06, would be in that blessed state, except of course that we don't have zero net immigration.

China's current TFR, based on figures from the 2010 census, is still being argued. Numbers as low as 1.4 have been put forward, but majority opinion among demographers seems to have settled in the zone 1.50-1.55, an international ranking of #184, below Russia but above Switzerland. And that's for the country as a whole: some of the big cities are recording *sensationally* low TFRs—Shanghai's 0.7, for example.

China's sex ratio at birth (SRB) has been noticeably skewed by selective abortion of females. At 1.133—that is, 1133 male children born for every 1000 female children—it is the highest in the world, though again the overall number hides big regional variations.

There is no general agreement about how much this matters. My own impression is: not much. (See my review of Mara Hvistendahl's *Unnatural Selection: Choosing Boys Over Girls, and the Consequences of a World Full of Men* here: http://www.johnderbyshire. com/Reviews/HumanSciences/unnaturalselection.html). Given its age-old tradition of female infanticide, China's SRB was likely always skewed to some degree.

The problem is anyway amenable to government action. South Korea, a country less authoritarian than China, brought their SRB down from a high level in the 1980s to near-normal a decade later by legislation and strict enforcement, and the residual excess of males will likely be "sopped up" by small changes in age differential at marriage.

Further, SRB is keyed to TFR, as SRB only diverges dramatically from normal at second or subsequent births. With a TFR down at 1.5, most births are first births.

If SRB is not a problem, though, TFR may be. As the cliché has it: China will get old before she gets rich. Demographic disaster?

I am sanguine. To quote from that world-historical bestseller *We Are Doomed*:

> If there is any demographic exceptionalism to be noted in the world, it is East Asia's: low birth rates, stiff resistance to mass immigration....
>
> It is a plausible general principle that, when the human race in its overall development comes to some kind of bridge, the first nation to cross the bridge successfully has a great advantage over other nations. Britain was the first nation to industrialize, and dominated world affairs for a century afterwards. If demographic decline is inevitable—which of course it is: the Earth must have *some* maximum carrying capacity—the first nation to get through the transition intact, and conquer the associated problems, will be at a huge advantage. On current showing, that will be Japan.

Followed by China...

...if there still *is* a China. For all the nationalistic bluster of recent years, Chinese nationhood has historically been a fragile thing. Lucian Pye's quip that China is "a civilization pretending to be a nation-state" captures the issue. China's history contains as much division as unification, and some of the unifications have been short—notably the first, which lasted a mere fifteen years.

Chinese civilization has many glories: national cohesion under stable, rational government has not been prominent among them.

The main problem raised by China's fast aging may in fact be not a shortage of workers so much as a shortage of security personnel to hold down the restive non-Chinese subject populations of Tibet and Eastern Turkestan (which, by the way, have not been subject to the stricter implementations of the one-child policy).

If China remains intact through the mid-21st century, it may be as only metropolitan China—the old Ming empire, plus Manchuria and Inner Mongolia, both of which have been (probably) irreversibly Sinified.

That would be a good outcome, comparable to the break-up of the U.S.S.R. A bad outcome would be another spell of core disintegration. A *really* bad one would be the strained, contested continuation of present control over what is, essentially, the Manchu Empire, minus Outer Mongolia.

In all three cases, though, and however you grade their relative desirabilities, the Chinese people—the historic ethnic bearers of Chinese civilization—would remain the overwhelmingly dominant population in metropolitan China.

From that point of view, the demographic disaster America would bring upon herself by continued mass immigration would be far worse than anything China might expect.

Chinese civilization would survive the loss of her border colonies, and even disintegration of the ethnic metropolitan core, as she has done many times before. That America's newer civilization would survive a population inflow of one or two hundred million souls from Latin America, Africa, India, Islamia, and East Asia (including of course China) is much less likely.

Demographics is, as I noted in that review of Mara Hvistendahl's book, surprisingly prone to prediction errors. But, so far as it is possible to see present trends leading to demographic disaster in China and America, I'll take theirs over ours.

* * *

This article can be read online at http://www.vdare.com/articles/ john-derbyshire-on-demographic-disasters-china-s-and-ours

The Dissident Right's Role— Unearthing "Hate Facts"

June 21, 2013

The forthcoming book of collected essays from Pierre Ryckmans— for more on which, see my current column "The Man Who Blew the Lid off Maoism," June 20, 2013 at *Taki's Magazine*—contains a nice little encomium to Fr. Laszlo Ladany, a Jesuit priest and scholar who, from 1953 to 1982, published a weekly bulletin titled *China News Analysis*.

Writing shortly before Fr. Ladany died in 1990, Ryckmans says this:

> Far away from the crude limelight of the media circus, he has enjoyed three decades of illustrious anonymity. All "China Watchers" used to read his newsletter with avidity; many stole from it—but generally they took great pains never to acknowledge their indebtedness or to mention his name....
>
> *China News Analysis* was compulsory reading for all those who wished to be informed of Chinese political developments: scholars, journalists, diplomats. In academe, however, its perusal among many political scientists was akin to what a drinking habit might be for an ayatollah, or an addiction to pornography for a bishop: it was a compulsive need that had to be indulged in secrecy. China experts gnashed their teeth as they read Ladany's incisive comments; they hated his clear-sightedness and cynicism; still, they could not afford to miss one single issue of his newsletter, for, however disturbing and scandalous his conclusions, the factual information he supplied was invaluable and irreplaceable.

By that point in Ryckmans' text, I was thinking of our own Steve Sailer, who claims on indirect but (it seems to me) convincing evidence that several of our bigfoot opinion journalists read his blog in the privacy of their chambers. I think Steve would object to "cynicism," though.

Why does Ryckmans think Fr. Ladany's newsletter was such compulsive reading for China experts?

> What made *China News Analysis* so infuriatingly indispensable was the very simple and original principle on which it was run (true originality is usually simple): all the information selected and examined in *China News Analysis* was drawn exclusively from official Chinese sources (press and radio)….
>
> What inspired his method was the observation that even the most mendacious propaganda must necessarily entertain some sort of relation with the truth; even as it manipulates and distorts the truth, it still needs originally to feed on it. Therefore, the untwisting of official lies, if skillfully effected, should yield a certain amount of straight facts. Needless to say, such an operation requires a *doigté* hardly less sophisticated than the chemistry which, in *Gulliver's Travels*, enabled the Grand Academicians of Lagado to extract sunbeams from cucumbers and food from excreta.

"Straight facts"… Hate facts. You can probably see where I'm headed with this. I'm going to try making an argument that we on the Dissident Right are performing a function not dissimilar to Fr. Ladany's work.

First let me just back off some and explain the situation of China watchers across the time span from Fr. Ladany starting his newsletter in 1953 to Mao Tse-tung's death in 1976.

China was at that time a closed country, like present-day North Korea. The precise degree of closed-ness varied with the ebb and flow of internal Chinese politics, but it was never easy to get a visa. Even if you got one, you could not move freely inside China. Chinese "minders" were assigned to you and managed your itinerary. Your contacts with ordinary Chinese people were very restricted.

(English politician and wit Clement Freud went to China with a parliamentary delegation in the late Mao years. At the welcoming banquet one of their hosts asked the parliamentarians what they would most like to see during their stay, assuming that they would opt for either a model commune, or a revolutionary ballet, or the award-winning hog bristle production brigade. Freud said brightly that he would *very much* like to see a labor camp. He was not invited back.)

It was extremely difficult for Western journalists to figure out what was going on at the high levels of Chinese politics. They had to do most of their watching from outside the country. There was a nest of them in Hong Kong, still a British Colony during that period; I was personally acquainted with some of them there in the early 1970s. They were very cynical, and drank a lot. Ryckmans:

In the course of his exhaustive surveys of Chinese official documentation, the analyst must absorb industrial quantities of the most indigestible stuff; reading Communist literature is akin to munching rhinoceros sausage, or to swallowing sawdust by the bucketful.... He must scan the arid wastes of the small print in the pages of the *People's Daily* and pounce upon those rare items of significance that lie buried under mountains of clichés. He must know how to milk substance and meaning out of flaccid speeches, hollow slogans and fanciful statistics; he must scavenge for needles in Himalayan-size haystacks.... He must crack the code of the Communist political jargon and translate into ordinary speech this secret language full of symbols, riddles, cryptograms, hints, traps, dark allusions and red herrings.

Now, I am not going to claim that extracting true hate facts from official U.S. government publications, or from reports in our mainstream media outlets, is as arduous as trying to fathom who did what to whom, and why, or even *where*, in (say) the Lin Biao incident. It can be something like that, though.

Just recently I did a *Taki's Magazine* column on sexual harassment in the U.S. military, concerning which the Defense Department recently put out a report. Rhinoceros sausage? Oh yeah.

> SARCs discuss DTM 11-063 requirements during briefings with new commanders and also emphasize this information with SAPR Program personnel (SAPR VA, SAPR POC, and SAPR Command Liaison) during training. All training material have been updated with newly implemented guidance regarding expedited transfers for Service members victims involved in Unrestricted reports of sexual assault.

Right. For extracting newsworthy facts from these bucketsful of sawdust, you really do need Fr. Ladany's dogged skills.

Take for example the odd fact that among active-duty military, "1.2% of men indicated they experienced unwanted sexual contact in 2012."[2] Given that 1.2 million of our active-duty military are male, that's 14½ thousand guys getting molested—forty a day. Good grief!

Corresponding numbers for active-duty military females are 6.1 percent of 205 thousand, which is 12½ thousand. So more guys than gals "experienced unwanted sexual contact in 2012."

What's up with *that?*

It's suggestive that when you look at the breakdown by service, the Navy comes out way ahead by incident rate at 2.7 percent, the other branches at 1.1 and below.[3] Closeness of confinement below decks? Or the Winston Churchill effect?

If you can figure out the answers to questions like that from the DoD report, you're a better analyst than I am. (Though I note, for

---

[2] Page 2 of http://www.sapr.mil/public/docs/research/2012_Workplace_and_Gender_Relations_Survey_of_Active_Duty_Members-Survey_Note_and_Briefing.pdf

[3] *Ibid.*, page 19

readers who might be thinking of joining the Navy, 6 PM to midnight on a Thursday is the time of greatest hazard.)[4]

And I'm just scratching the surface here. Try tackling the following question:

- *For all these unwanted sexual contacts (sexual touching, attempted or actual sexual intercourse, attempted or actual other penetrations), what are the breakdowns by race?*

This comes to mind because of the extraordinary differentials for interracial rape and sexual assault in society at large recorded in a typical year by the National Crime Victimization Survey. In 2008, for instance, black-on-white numbers for these crimes were 19 thousand, while white-on-black were too few for the sampling methodology to process.[5]

Is this pattern repeated in the military?

That you may not know. It is Hateful just to ask. If the numbers are even gathered, they are kept in a filing drawer at the Pentagon under a higher security clearance than ICBM targeting codes.

The booze-fuddled hacks I used to hang out with in the Kowloon bars back in the day had a better chance of finding out what Mao Tse-tung had for breakfast than I have of getting interracial sexual-assault stats for the U.S. Navy.

Ryckmans:

Without an ability to decipher non-existent inscriptions written in invisible ink on blank pages, no-one should ever dream of

---

[4] Page 487 of http://sapr.mil/public/docs/reports/FY12_DoD_SAPRO_Annual_Report_on_Sexual_Assault-VOLUME_ONE.pdf

[5] Table 42 of http://www.bjs.gov/content/pub/pdf/cvus0802.pdf

analyzing the nature and reality of Chinese communism. Very few people have mastered this demanding discipline, and, with good reason, they generally acknowledge Father Ladany as their doyen.

"Analyzing the nature and reality" of modern Western society is largely a matter of unearthing Hate Facts. For this, special skills are needed. They are in all too short supply.

Could we perhaps start up some training courses?

* * *

This article can be read online at http://www.vdare.com/articles/ john-derbyshire-on-the-dissident-right-s-role-in-producing-hate-facts

On the Origins of the Amnesty/Immigration Surge Bill: Getting to Treason

June 29, 2013

Now that the Amnesty and Immigration Surge Bill has been voted up by the U.S. Senate, it is instructive to step back and take a look at its origins.

The sheer amount of legislative effort here has, after all, been tremendous. At twelve hundred pages, the bill is almost as long as *War and Peace*—sixty times the length of the original U.S. Constitution. Such heroic labors! Why? What have been the motivations of the bill's authors and movers?

I thought I might gain some insight into this from a close reading of Ryan Lizza's piece "Getting to Maybe: Inside the Gang of Eight's Immigration Deal," in the June 24th *New Yorker*.

Lizza is the magazine's Washington correspondent. His article gives all the personal dynamics of the Senate's taking up the bill and passing it through the Judiciary Committee. (It does not of course take us all the way to this week's final passage.)

"Getting to Maybe" is written with flawless professional objectivity, the writer himself almost invisible, offering no commentary, no opinion, and no sign of any engagement with the underlying issue.

Even when the protagonists in the story are at their most mendacious or obnoxious, Lizza resists the temptation to add any critical or ironic coloring to his narrative, allowing their words to speak for themselves.

He writes for example of the first bonding between John McCain and Chuck Schumer, in meetings last fall to preserve the Senate's filibuster rule:

> McCain agreed that the meetings built trust between him and Schumer. "The reason why I enjoyed working with Ted Ken-

94

nedy is because Ted was always good to his word," he said. "And so is Chuck."

Any regular reader of *VDARE.com*, recalling Ted Kennedy's barefaced lies about the 1965 immigration bill he championed, would have sprayed coffee over page 47 of the *New Yorker* at that point, but Lizza passes on without comment.

Likewise with Lizza's coverage of the Heritage-Richwine flap last month.

McCain could hardly contain himself as he recited the story of how the Heritage report backfired. "Ka-boom!" he yelled. "That was a gift from God.... But, yeah, those low-I.Q. Hispanics, I'll tell ya, that was really revealing to me, I had no idea." McCain, who is of Irish heritage, added, "We've always known that about the Irish."

Ha ha ha ha! Never mind that a young scholar's career was destroyed for having, *in a Harvard doctoral dissertation*, tried to introduce some quantitative facts about human capital into the immigration debate.

Politics proverbially ain't beanbag, but I don't think politicians are supposed to take quite so much pleasure in inflicting collateral casualties. On Lizza's account, John McCain really does seem to be an extremely unpleasant person.

The passage in Lizza's piece that got everyone's attention was the quote he included from a Rubio aide that: "There are American workers who, for lack of a better term, can't cut it. There shouldn't be a presumption that every American worker is a star performer."

When Rubio's people pushed back indignantly against that quote, Lizza quietly released the full transcript of his notes, according to which a second Rubio aide had chimed in:

Rubio Aide 2: But the same is true for the high-skilled workers.

Rubio Aide 1: Yes, and the same is true across every sector, in government, in everything.

Mickey Kaus summarized the Rubio aides' view of American workers:

There's a reason unemployed Americans are unemployed. They aren't star performers. Screw 'em. We're bringing in workers from abroad!

No news to anyone on this side of the issue, but nice to see the truth aired by writers closer to the mainstream.

There are one or two soft brown spots in Lizza's piece, where he takes conventional immigration cant at face value. This I think is only ignorance, though, not any propagandistic intent on Lizza's part.

H-1B visas...allow companies like Google and Facebook to bring highly skilled engineers from abroad to work for them temporarily in America.

As if "abroad" were the only place where such engineers could be found; as if there were anything "temporary" about their residence here.

These minor lapses aside, Lizza's cold, neutral prose works very well, impressing on the reader better than any polemic could the shallow motives of the players, their pathetic innumeracy, and their near-total ignorance of immigration realities.

Republicans looked at the [2012] polling results: "a steady decline from Bush to me to Mitt," McCain said.

The actual decline in Hispanics voting for Republican presidential candidates, 2004-08-12, has been from 40 percent of 6.0 percent of the electorate to 27 percent of 8.4 percent. That is to say, from 2.4 percent of the overall electorate, to 2.3 percent. As we've been saying for years, it's nothing that could not easily be swamped by modest increases in the non-Hispanic white vote.

Nobody expects U.S. Senators to be philosopher-kings—well, *I* don't—but it is very depressing to see how little of the real, fact-based discussions on immigration policy conducted here and elsewhere has penetrated senatorial heads.

As it happens, I sat down with Lizza's piece just after reading all through that epic, much-circulated comment thread on Tyler Cowen's website. Peter Schaeffer is the, ah, star performer here:

> The Economic Report of the President (EROP), Table B-35 gives total employment at 143.305 million. Table B-47 gives hours worked at 33.7 per week. A little math gives total hours at 251.127 billion. That's rather close to the Conference Board data.
>
> National Health Expenditures appear to be in the $3 trillion range. [Peter goes into some critical discussion of this number. Then:] If $3 trillion is the correct health care number, then $12 per hour is about right. You can tweak the number up and down a bit by changing your estimate of health care spending, but it's going to be in that range.

That's key quantitative data. Total hours worked per annum in the U.S.A.: a quarter trillion. Total healthcare expenditures: three trillion. Healthcare costs per hour worked: $12. (Other commenters raise objections: Schaeffer fields them very deftly.)

> The minimum wage is $7.25 per hour. If a minimum wage worker paid 100% of his income in taxes (or health care premiums), America would still lose $4.75 on health care costs alone.

Did anyone ever think to do this rather straightforward piece of arithmetic before? In particular, did any of the researchers attached to any of the Senators named in Ryan Lizza's piece think to do it? If one of them had, would he have been able to hammer it through a thick senatorial skull?

By contrast we get this from Chuck Schumer, on illegal immigrants:

> I'm not saying they're bad people. I would do the same thing
> if my mother and children were starving in Oaxaca Province.

So far as I can discover there has been no famine in Mexico since the 15th century. Life expectancy in Oaxaca, according to Wikipedia, "is 71.7 for men and 77.4 for women, just under the national average," while: "Ninety five percent of Oaxaca's population receives health care from one or more government programs." Modern Mexico is a middle-class country, with per capita GDP $15,300, twice that of Ukraine and three times Syria's.

Quantitative facts like these—on voting percentages, the external costs of "cheap" labor, living standards in people-exporting countries—are easy to find. Why are they so easy to ignore?

I return to my opening question: What is driving this stupendous legislative effort? There is money, to be sure: When George Soros, Sheldon Adelson, Mark Zuckerberg, and Michael Bloomberg are all pushing hard on one side of an issue, things will happen. Immigration romanticism? Probably, given the prominence in the Gang of Eight of Chuck Schumer, an Ashkenazi huddled-masses romantic from Central Casting. The Cold Civil War—one great section of U.S. whites seeking to marginalize and crush another section? Undoubtedly: listen to them crowing at the prospect of whites becoming a minority.

There is something else, though, that I think comes through clearly from Ryan Lizza's article.

Back in the 1970s I had a colleague who was a hi-fi buff. He talked about hi-fi a lot; he subscribed to hi-fi magazines, and read them in his coffee break; he spent much of his disposable income on hi-fi equipment. In the fullness of time we got sufficiently friendly that I was invited to his apartment. Riding the cab over there, I naturally wondered what I would hear on the hi-fi buff's hi-fi. Mozart's 19th String Quartet? The Dallas Callas? The Mormon Tabernacle Choir?

What I heard was Herb Alpert and his Tijuana Brass, along with some similar easy-listening elevator music. Thence the life lesson: For some people, process matters more than result, form more than content, the container more than what is contained.

The overwhelming impression given by Lizza's account is of a group of men (there seem to be no gyno-American Senators involved with immigration) obsessed with legislative process over any concern for national interest or any desire to engage with quantitative data.

In Schumer's case, this is no surprise. The senior U.S. senator from my state boasted when campaigning in 1998 that he had "a passion to legislate."

That's your problem right there.

* * *

This article can be read online at http://www.vdare.com/articles/ john-derbyshire-on-the-origins-of-the-amnestyimmigration-surge- bill-getting-to-treason

On "Contact Theory"—
Ignorance is Bliss, But Familiarity Breeds...
What, Exactly?

July 5, 2013

On February 3rd 1954 the British Cabinet, under Prime Minister Winston Churchill, discussed the issue of the fast-swelling nonwhite population of the U.K. That population then stood at 40,000, most of them blacks from the Caribbean, eighty percent having arrived in the previous six years.

Sir David Maxwell Fyfe, the Home Secretary (i.e. Attorney General, approximately) weighed the pros and cons of controlling the inflow by legislation. By imposing controls, said Sir David, as reported in the abbreviated language of Cabinet minutes:

> "We should be reversing age-long tradition that British subjects have right of entry to mother-country of Empire. We should offend liberals, also sentimentalists." Accordingly, "on balance, scale of the problem is such that we shouldn't take these risks today." He finished with a shrewd, cynical thrust: "The coloured populations are resented in Liverpool, Paddington and other areas—*by those who come into contact with them. But those who don't are apt to take liberal view.*"

My emphasis. I took that extract from *Family Britain, 1951-1957,* the second volume of David Kynaston's social history of the post-WW2 United Kingdom.

(To the degree that Sir David Maxwell Fyfe is remembered at all today it is for his response to Member of Parliament—and promiscuous bisexual—Robert Boothby when Boothby was lobbying for reform of Britain's homosexuality laws: "I am not going down in history as the man who made sodomy legal.")

100

Curiously, the year 1954 also saw the publication of Gordon All-port's book *The Nature of Prejudice*, which is generally credited with having unleashed "Contact Theory" on an unsuspecting world.

Contact Theory takes a point of view opposite to Sir David Maxwell Fyfe's. It argues that group prejudices and stereotypes are a result of isolation and ignorance. If persons from different groups are brought together, says the Contact Theorist, they will see the falseness of their prejudices and embrace the "psychic unity of mankind."

Contact Theory is one of the foundation stones of the modern cult of Diversity.

To be fair to Gordon Allport, *The Nature of Prejudice* presented Contact Theory in a subtle and qualified form. Allport repeatedly stressed, for example, that the individuals in contact need to see themselves as being on the same social level for the theory to work its magic: "occupational contacts with Negroes *of equal status* tend to make for lessened prejudice," etc. (page 276, Allport's emphasis).

Subsequent social science research, notably Robert Putnam's much-discussed 2006 paper, further diluted Contact Theory down to well-nigh homeopathic levels. There is a good discussion of the theory's current status in Chapter IV of Russell Nieli's book *Wounds That Will Not Heal*, which I reviewed for *VDARE.com* (see p. 75).

Sir David's observation that familiarity breeds rancor while ignorance is multicultural bliss seems oddly up-to-date. Here for example was I, writing after last November's election:

> In the state of Mississippi...89 percent of whites voted for Romney; in the state of Alabama, it was 84 percent. In the state of Maine, on the other hand, only 40 percent of whites voted for Romney; in Vermont, only 33 percent.

The immigration debates in British Cabinets of the early 1950s are full of similar echoes of today's immigration debates. Try this:

The main cause of this sudden inflow of blacks is of course the Welfare State. So long as the antiquated rule obtains that any British subject can come into this country without any limitation at all, these people will pour in to take advantage of our social services and other amenities, and we shall have no protection at all.

That was Lord Salisbury writing to a colleague in March 1954. Or this:

It was hardly surprising that all efforts to persuade the West Indian governments themselves to retard emigration ran up against the rock of their self-interest; they were effectively exporting unemployment and, when the immigrants sent money back to their families, importing capital.

That was from Chapter 4 of Andrew Roberts' *Eminent Churchillians*, which gives full coverage of the topic, and of the determination on the part of mid-1950s British governments to do nothing at all about it.

The first restrictions on settlement by "British subjects"—that is, people from the old British Empire—were introduced in 1961. "By that time, however," as Roberts says, "the pass had been sold."

To me personally, David Kynaston's books about postwar Britain are especially fascinating. They begin precisely where my existence did, around VE Day. The first volume, *Austerity Britain*, covers 1945-51; the second, noted above, is *Family Britain*, covering 1951-57. The third, just published over there, is *Modernity Britain, 1957-1959*.

It's a very engrossing thing, to read social history precisely keyed to one's own lifespan. Words and names loaded with strange power, that seemed, to one's childish understanding, to loom up suddenly, inexplicably, out of the fog of adult concerns, are here seen in their humdrum context: Johnnie Ray! Formica! Polio! Wilfred Pickles!

There are some surprises. Working my way through the first volume, I was curious to see which event in the world at large was the first of which I had any memory at all. Astonishingly, for a person as severely fashion-challenged as myself, it was the New Look, which I remember my mother and her housewife friends talking about. Psychologists tell us that our first memories form around age 2½, so I suppose I am remembering late 1947. Good grief!

Time and again, though, working through Kynaston's pages, I am reminded that I belong to the last generation of whites to grow up in a monoracial nation. Because nonwhites were concentrated in a few big cities, Sir David Maxwell Fyfe's rule applied. From *Family Britain*:

> Gallup in April 1955 asked, "Do you think it is right or wrong for people to refuse to work with coloured men or women?", to which only 12 percent thought it was right, whereas 79 percent thought it wrong. (In the same poll, to the question "Do you personally know or have you known any coloured people?", 58 percent replied in the negative.)

The inhabitants of our own sleepy country town must have been solidly in the 58 percent.

The racial vacuum was to some degree filled by the narcissism of small differences, with class of course the main marker. Kynaston:

> Robert Roberts...identified an "English proletarian caste system" that divided working-class people living or working in the same place; it is clear that this system was still alive and well after the Second World War. "The East Enders could be incredibly snobbish and class-conscious in their social gradings"....

It sure was: *that*, I remember well. Every town and district had a "rough" neighborhood where respectable people didn't venture; every street in a "decent" working-class neighborhood had a problem family: house dirty, husband work-shy, wife coarse and boozy, kids numerous and feral.

In accordance with Sir David Maxwell Fyfe's dictum, we grew up racial egalitarians, so that by college age we were marching against Apartheid and cheering on the U.S. Civil Rights movement.

On the other hand, *contra* Sir David, the college-age kids of today, raised in multiculturalism, are also mostly racial egalitarians, if perhaps a tad more so in Maine and Vermont than in Mississippi and Alabama. The power of childhood indoctrination? Youthful idealism trumping reality? The tame docility of a supervised, playgrouped generation raised by helicopter parents?

I don't know. I do like to think, though, that the experience of growing up around human nature in all its fullness—the good, the bad, the exemplary and the appalling—all packed into one's own ethny, forms a better foundation for a mature adult view of human group differences than the coloring-book simplicities of the Diversity cult.

What do they think, this new generation we've raised, as they see the East Asian kids packing the AP Algebra classes, black flash mobs on YouTube, Amerids vegetating in scholastic mediocrity, the endless scroll of Jewish names in law, the media, the intelligentsia,…?

When they have cleared their minds of cant at last, what will take its place: cool realism, or warm rancor?

Perhaps Contact Theorists, if there are any left, could look into the matter.

* * *

This article can be read online at http://www.vdare.com/articles/ john-derbyshire-on-contact-theory-ignorance-is-bliss-but-familiarity-breeds-what-exactly

The Voter Demographic
That Dare Not Speak Its Name

August 8, 2013

I can't say I'm a very keen fan of the *Parade* mini-magazine that comes with my Sunday *New York Post*. My wife pulls it out to read over her breakfast while I go directly to op-ed articles in the main newspaper—thumb-sucking pieces about the collapse of Detroit or the prospects for Syria.

Not that I mind *Parade* at all. On balance I'll allow it's a Good Thing. For those like Mrs. Derbyshire who take it at face value, it offers generally sound advice on matters like health, parenting, and household finances, in among harmless celebrity gossip, nostalgia pieces for the older readers, and uplifting stories about citizens who have triumphed over adversity.

For those of us with a more coldly sociological eye, *Parade* is a window into the interests and concerns of those sensible tens of millions of Americans who, like the great Warren G. Harding (according to historian Paul Johnson), do not believe that politics are "very important or that people should get excited about them or allow them to penetrate too far into their everyday lives."

So no, I don't mind *Parade*; it's just that its content doesn't usually interest me much.

But last week's issue was an exception. The cover showed super-celebrity Oprah Winfrey and movie actor Forest Whitaker, with a short caption telling me that these two are starring in a film about a White House butler during the Civil Rights era.

This was interesting to me because, during my 1980s campaign to Americanize myself, one of the books I read and enjoyed was *Forty-Two Years in the White House*, the 1934 memoir by White House usher Ike Hoover.

Hoover had served under all the Presidents from Benjamin Harrison ("Very seldom did he work after lunch") to FDR, about whom

Hoover was diplomatically silent. He is an invaluable source on such things as the smoking habits of the Presidents and First Ladies: McKinley the most intense smoker (cigars only), Mrs. Coolidge the only First Lady who smoked ("and she never did so in public").

Thus primed, I was mildly curious about the Winfrey-Whitaker movie, which is scheduled for release August 16th. So I read the *Parade* piece, in which the magazine interviews Winfrey, Whitaker, and director Lee Daniels. ["Oprah Winfrey, Forest Whitaker Talk Lee Daniels' *The Butler*, Racism, and the N-word," Katherine Heintzelman, July 31, 2013.]

Titled *The Butler*, the movie is a fictionalized account of the career of another White House servant, Eugene Allen, who served in the White House from 1952 to 1986.

Whitaker is the Allen character (under a different name). Winfrey plays his wife, Gloria. "We took a lot of liberties with Gloria," Winfrey tells *Parade*. Uh-oh. Robin Williams plays Eisenhower; Jane Fonda is Nancy Reagan. Uh-*oh*.

To judge from the *Parade* interview, *The Butler* is not an assemblage of amusing or instructive anecdotes about The Presidents in Ike Hoover style. Instead, it is black grievance porn.

So is the *Parade* interview itself.

> *Parade*: Do you think that young people today know enough about the civil rights movement?
>
> Winfrey: They don't know diddly-squat. Diddly-squat!

Later:

> Whitaker: The movie deals with the valuation of life, too. Like, whose life is valuable?... In terms of today, *Fruitvale Station* is playing, about the shooting of Oscar Grant in the Oakland BART station....
>
> Winfrey: And the shooting of Trayvon Martin.

Soon no doubt to be a major motion picture, perhaps directed by Lee Daniels. Or perhaps Mr. Daniels is planning a movie about one of the innumerable whites and Asians murdered by blacks? Ha ha ha ha ha!

The Deplorable Word? We get a whole column and a half on it.

> Winfrey: It's hard to be loose-lipped with that word. I always think of the millions of people who heard that as their last word as they were hanging from a tree.

Millions! As Kathy Shaidle has pointed out, the actual number of persons lynched, 1882-1968, was tallied by the Tuskegee Institute at 4,743, of whom 1,297—that's 27 percent—were white. Lynching-wise, Ms. Winfrey doesn't know diddly-squat.

Her blithe lack of self-awareness adds some touches of unintentional hilarity to the interview, though.

> Winfrey: Lee was relentless. I remember being on my mountain in Maui, where I go to try to restore myself. And he called saying: "You need to get ready, because you *are* Gloria."

Of course, having your own Hawaiian mountain can't erase the memory of earlier indignities:

> Winfrey: You know, my mother was a maid....

So what? Millions of white people could say the same thing. Has Ms. Winfrey never seen an episode of *Downton Abbey?* My own mother's first employment was as a domestic servant. Who the hell does Oprah Winfrey think she is?

Nevertheless, for all its narcissism, ignorance, moon-booted guilt-mongering, and picking at ancient scabs, the *Parade* Winfrey-Whitaker-Daniels interview illustrated an important point about race in the U.S.A.: the fact that black Americans have an *epic*.

The forebears who were domestic servants; the segregated drinking fountains; the lynchings and humiliations; Jim Crow and slavery; the Middle Passage; the original African paradise; the names of the victims and martyrs; it all forms an epic, a historical drama. Much of it is inaccurate, of course, and some of it is empty nonsense, but that's always the way with epics.

Any people that nurses a common identity has an epic. The British had one when I was a kid, organized around the monarchs, whose names we memorized:

> *Henry the Fourth for himself took the crown; Henry the Fifth pulled the French king down; Henry the Sixth lost his father's gains; Edward of York laid hold of the reins....*

Like the black American epic, the British one was deformed somewhat to give it a moral shape. I don't recall hearing about the Potato Famine or the Amritsar Massacre in school history lessons. Again, though, that's the way with epics.

The Chinese, who have been nursing their identity longer than anyone, have a multilayered epic that does not always agree with itself. Living there thirty years ago I had to try not to smile when some colleague steeped in the Maoist ethos spoke of the darkness and oppression of the Old Society and then, five minutes later, extolled the glories of China's ancient civilization.

Do white Americans have an epic? We used to have one, in fact more than one. George Orwell glimpsed them from his childhood reading:

> One other imaginary country that I acquired early in life was called America. If I pause on the word "America," and, deliberately putting aside the existing reality, call up my childhood vision of it, I see two pictures—composite pictures, of course, from which I am omitting a good deal of the detail.
>
> One is of a boy sitting in a whitewashed stone schoolroom. He wears braces [JD: =suspenders] and has patches on his shirt, and if it is summer he is barefooted. In the corner of the school room there is a bucket of drinking water with a dipper.

The boy lives in a farm-house, also of stone and also white-washed, which has a mortgage on it. He aspires to be President, and is expected to keep the woodpile full. Somewhere in the background of the picture, but completely dominating it, is a huge black Bible.

The other picture is of a tall, angular man, with a shapeless hat pulled down over his eyes, leaning against a wooden paling and whittling at a stick. His lower jaw moves slowly but ceaselessly. At very long intervals he emits some piece of wisdom such as "A woman is the orneriest critter there is, 'ceptin' a mule," or "When you don't know a thing to do, don't do a thing"; but more often it is a jet of tobacco juice that issues from the gap in his front teeth.

Between them those two pictures summed up my earliest impression of America. And of the two, the first—which, I suppose, represented New England, the other representing the South—had the stronger hold upon me. [*Riding Down from Bangor*, 1946.]

To me, that second picture of Orwell's sounds more like the West than the South.

It was the West that, in the middle decades of the 20th century, looked like providing the most compelling element of the American epic: the Wild West. Even across the Pond in 1950s England, the cowboy, the saloon, the six-shooter, the tepee, the covered wagon, were as familiar to us as our own humdrum surroundings. Now *that* was an epic!

Nowadays, following the peculiar inversion our civilization has undergone in the past forty years, white Americans have an *anti*-epic. The great dramatic events are all there, adjusted to fit in a moral framework; but we are the villains of the story. The West was won not by doughty pioneers braving the unknown, but by homicidal gangs, by land-grab wars against Mexico, by the massacre of Indians, and by the conscription of Chinese coolie labor. When was the last *non-ironic* Western movie made?

(It's the same in Britain. No longer brushed under the national carpet, the Potato Famine and the Amritsar Massacre are now major elements of the school history syllabus. Probably Amritsar is better known to British schoolchildren than Waterloo.)

That is the background to current discussions about the white vote: Its size, its direction, the morality and practicality of Republican candidates making direct appeals to it. Whiteness is *shameful*. The proper posture of white Americans and white politicians is guilty abnegation.

Hence the shocked responses in the comment thread to *New York Times* columnist Ross Douthat's recent ruminations on the white vote. ["Republicans, White Voters, and Racial Polarization," *New York Times,* August 6, 2013.] To write about whites as a collectivity, in any context other than that of historical crimes, is illegitimate.

Hence also the inadequacy of Douthat's analysis. He writes:

> Energizing "ascendant" constituencies while pushing working-class whites toward the Republicans has represented a form of "positive polarization" for the Democrats, since it's left them with a presidential-level majority that they did not enjoy before.

But working class whites have not been so much pushed towards the Republicans as pushed out of politics altogether. That's why so many of them went missing last November. They may have been pushed *towards* the Republicans, but the GOP gave no indication it wanted them.

If, after an hour of play, nobody has passed you the ball, you may as well quit the game—walk off the pitch, go home, watch some reality TV. And that's what the white working-class vote has done. No politician passes the ball to them because no politician wants it thought that he's singling them out for positive attention. That would be…oh, you know.

No, not even Senator Jeff Sessions, hero of the recent Senate "debate" on the Eight Gangsters' Amnesty/Immigration Surge bill. His recent powerful statement "How the GOP Can Do the Right Thing on Immigration—and Win" faltered at exactly this point:

> The GOP lost the election—as exit polls clearly show— because it hemorrhaged support from middle- and low-income Americans of all backgrounds. ["Sessions to Republicans: GOP Elite View on Immigration Is 'Nonsense'," *Weekly Standard*, July 29th.]

Support for the GOP from "middle- and low-income Americans" of backgrounds other than non-Hispanic white is so inconsequential— small-minority percentages of minority percentages—it is absurd to speak of it "hemorrhaging."

Senator Sessions is speaking diplomatically, of course, as he must, and I do not mean to belittle his magnificent efforts and stirring rhetoric against the Schumer-Rubio bill. But that's the point: he must speak of "all backgrounds," although he surely knows that the hemorrhaging was of whites—the demographic that dare not speak its shameful name.

It is an extraordinary situation; ethnomasochism is an extraordinary state of mind; the marginalizing of non-elite whites—a substantial majority of the population!—by the Cultural Marxists is an extraordinary achievement.

That is the environment we work in, though. The only suggestion anyone has come up with for getting working-class whites back on the field and playing with the GOP team, is economic populism.

Sean Trende:

> Ultimately, the basic prescription for the GOP is a healthy dose of economic populism. This includes a lot of changes

Democrats would presumably enjoy, such as jettisoning the pro-big-business, Wall Street-style conservatism that characterized the Romney campaign for something authentically geared more toward downscale voters. ["Demographics and the GOP, Part IV," *Real Clear Politics*, July 2, 2013.]

Douthat thinks there might even be trans-racial appeal:

If Republicans interpret Trende's analysis correctly and set out to increase their margins with working class whites by developing a more inclusive and populist vision on economic policy, then they will probably ultimately win more Hispanic and even African-American votes as well.

Possibly so; but economic populism has already had a good airing this past quarter-century—Buchanan, Perot—and been found not merely wanting, but *racist*.

However, a *focused* economic-populist approach could yield some electoral dividends among disaffected whites. Patriotic immigration reform is likely the easiest policy to advance, enjoying as it does widespread support among both whites and blacks—and, according to Trende, not alienating Hispanics as much as GOP consultants fear.

This one issue might stir the non-elite white electorate into wakefulness.

The trick is to find a viable GOP presidential candidate who is not perfectly clueless about it.

* * *

This article can be read online at http://www.vdare.com/articles/ john-derbyshire-on-the-voter-demographic-that-dare-not-speak-its- name

Lowry on Lincoln: A Safe Whiggish Pep Talk for GOP Loyalists—Useless on the Real Issues

August 22, 2013

As the comfort and security of life in advanced societies have improved so sensationally this past half-century, the scope of topics considered respectable for public debate has narrowed, almost to the point where only a single set of ideas about the organization of society is now tolerated.

This process has had dire effects on party politics, which is now extremely boring, since there is so little to discuss.

To be interested in party politics nowadays, other than as a clash of personalities—which anyway happens much more *within* parties than *between* them—is a puzzling but harmless eccentricity, like stamp collecting.

But well within living memory—within *my* memory, darn it— there were mighty differences of political opinion. Thus the Labour Party politicians who came to power in Britain after WW2 were genuine socialists who believed in "the common ownership of the means of production, distribution and exchange." Those very words were printed on your Labour Party membership card.

They meant it, too. Great swathes of British industry were put under state control by Labour. Healthcare became a government department. Sturdy, roomy houses with big gardens were built at public expense and rented to the poor. (I grew up in one of them.) The dismantling of the British Empire was begun.

Political parties embodied vast differences in outlook. Socialist firebrand Aneurin Bevan (Labour) nationalized healthcare and built all those houses, until—to borrow Margaret Thatcher's handy expression—he ran out of other people's money. The Marquess of Salisbury (in the following Conservative government) expelled an African prince from a British colony for marrying a white woman.

Nowadays Britain has three big social-democratic parties whose policies differ only in microscopic details. The current Prime Minister, David Cameron, recently laid aside all other parliamentary business—lackluster economy, floods of immigrant terrorists and criminals, a swelling entitlements crisis—to push through *the legalization of homosexual marriage*. This Prime Minister belongs to the *Conservative* Party!

In the U.S.A., where explicit socialism never had much purchase and politics was traditionally sectional, increasing geographical homogeneity has brought about a similar result. The stuff of inter-party contention now is tiny points of taxation policy and healthcare reform, and noisy but inconsequential (in the sense that everyone understands nothing will happen) differences on social issues.

A friend quipped to me recently that the GOP is just the Democratic Party with an anti-abortion plank. That's depressingly close to the truth.

This increasing uniformity of political opinion is enforced by an ever more vigilant policing of the language, as foretold by, of course, George Orwell:

> "Don't you see [Winston Smith's colleague explains to him] that the whole aim of Newspeak is to narrow the range of thought? In the end we shall make thoughtcrime literally impossible, because there will be no words in which to express it." [*Nineteen Eighty-Four*, Chapter V.]

The recent career of the phrase "self-deportation" illustrates Orwell's point. A mere two or three years ago it described the mildest, least proactive style of immigration law enforcement. Now it is a "horrific" outrage against human rights, according to…the Chairman of the Republican National Committee! ["CORRECTED: GOP CHIEF: Mitt Romney's 'Self-Deportation' Quote Was 'Horrific'," Brett LoGiurato, *Business Insider,* August 16, 2013.]

(I have tried to float the term "hate creep" for this general linguistic narrowing.)

It would be natural to expect that the less-enthusiastic half of the social-democratic stage donkey would be shedding membership. And this seems to be happening.

In Britain, the Conservative Party—the one that pushed homosexual marriage through parliament—has been "hemorrhaging" members, according to one report.

Here in the U.S.A., it is now widely understood that the GOP's failure to capture the Presidency from a weak incumbent in 2012 was due to great numbers of conservative white voters having stayed at home, apparently seeing no point in voting for the donkey's front legs rather than the back.

Of course, an important difference between the countries is that conservative British voters have a plausible new party to attach themselves to. America's Dissident Right, by contrast, has yet to coalesce into any kind of political force, although the votes are certainly out there, if some figure of political genius could find a way to speak to them.

Given all of this, party-political literature is now unreadable. The poor hack reviewer who is confronted with a book plainly designed as a pep talk to one half or other of the stage donkey is bound to experience a strong gravitational pull from the direction of the liquor cabinet.

That was the situation I found myself in when the proprietor of this website urged me to review *National Review* Editor Rich Lowry's book *Lincoln Unbound*. I have, with my own ears, before my expulsion from *NR*, heard Lowry say that party politics is his main enthusiasm.

Lowry is a GOP supporter. Party members currently need cheering up. Abraham Lincoln was a Republican. Hey!

So I expected the book to be a snoozer. In fact it's not bad. This is mainly because the first eighty percent of it is a straightforward biography of Lincoln, an interesting man who lived in interesting times, about whom it's hard to write anything dull.

People have, of course, different attitudes towards Lincoln. Look, I hang out on the Dissident Right. *I know this.* Please don't write to tell me.

Some months ago in fact, following a column about my Civil War self-education project, a kind reader sent me Thomas DiLorenzo's books on Lincoln (*The Real Lincoln: A New Look at Abraham Lincoln, His Agenda, and an Unnecessary War* and *Lincoln Unmasked: What You're Not Supposed to Know About Dishonest Abe*), and I read them with keen attention. As a natural contrarian, I'm glad to have read the books, and DiLorenzo has a fine vigorous style; but I'm bound to say I don't think he lays much of a glove on Lincoln.

Not, at any rate, on the Lincoln of the scholarly biographers. DiLorenzo's "revelations"—Lincoln was a railroad booster! He suspended *habeas corpus!* The Emancipation Proclamation was a military-political chess move!—are all cheerfully admitted by the serious biographers I have read.

I don't doubt they might be startling to someone who only knows the sage, saintly Lincoln of popular culture. But a great many things will be startling to you if you don't read serious books.

Lincoln's career and personality have now been so worked over by biographers that the main contours are not in doubt, minor scholarly quibbles aside.

That is not to say that the South had no case, that Lincoln handled secession wisely, or that the Civil War was necessary. I think the war could and should have been avoided. I further think that if the principals—including Lincoln—had been able, in 1860-61, to anticipate the destruction and massacres of those four years, they would have striven mightily to prevent them.

But alas, history doesn't work like that. As Kierkegaard pointed out, it can only be understood backwards, but it has to be lived through forwards.

Lowry mentions DiLorenzo's work in passing, but dismisses that author's principal book as "rancid"—displaying the horror that a conventional, unimaginative person feels towards strong opinions. For Lincoln's life he seems to depend mainly on Allen Guelzo's biography.

It's not a bad choice, if you discount some for Guelzo's Lincoln-groupie tendencies. (About which I had words to say in my review of Guelzo's *Gettysburg* here: http://spectator.org/articles/55392/field-dreams. And if you don't want to read Guelzo's 500-odd pages on Lincoln, you can get the essence of it by listening to his Great Courses lectures.)

Thus we get 200 pages of good-quality prose on this very interesting President, his life and times. There is nothing new in it; Lowry does some mild "spinning" here and there towards his ultimate goal; and there is some mean snideness towards the South. ("What kind of country would it be if people felt compelled to get right with Jefferson Davis or John C. Calhoun?" asks Lowry, as if these were not Americans of the highest principle and integrity.) That aside, I couldn't find much to object to in this biographical eighty percent of *Lincoln Unbound*.

Then, in the final chapter, we get the GOP pep talk; and here, sure enough, the readability drops off like a coastal shelf. The main thrust here: the U.S.A. in general, and the Republican Party in particular, needs to recapture the Whiggish spirit of personal and commercial striving, as exemplified by Abraham Lincoln.

There are some quick cheap ripostes you can make here. Lincoln's career in commerce was brief and (to put it mildly) inglorious. He made his living from minor government jobs, then from lawyering. His ambition, which everyone who knew him remarked on, was all directed towards politics. He would likely have done well for himself in the U.S.S.R.

Lincoln's heart was in the right place, though. He had a keen, well-earned sense of what one of his near-contemporaries called "the idiocy of rural life," which any curious, reflective person in that time and place must surely have shared. The financial and infrastructure projects he favored improved the country greatly; and if—hat tip to Prof. DiLorenzo—they enriched Lincoln and his friends, I personally won't complain. You may disagree with Lincoln's reading of the Founders, but there is no doubt he revered them and interpreted them sincerely, to the best of his ability...and so on. I count myself pro-Lincoln.

Lincoln's arguments are all pretty much won, though. Hardly any of us are farmers; and Jeffersonian agrarianism, if not quite dead, is not a political force, nor likely to become one. For better or worse, we are a single, very big country, under a strong central government.

More than that: We now have a clearer picture of the downsides of democratic capitalism—its destructive effects on culture and social life.

More, and worse, yet: The quantitative human sciences are bringing the human essence into ever-sharper focus, and casting doubt on the post-1965 ideological consensus about human group equality. Lowry urges us to a project of "recovery...of the American character and of bourgeois virtues." It is highly probable that that character and those virtues cannot exist other than in a predominantly north-European population, which we shall soon no longer have.

Lowry's prescriptions are good uplifting stuff—embrace innovation and consumer choice! reform entitlements! crack down on government unions! elevate the culture! But they leave the reader reflecting that there is something systemic, a level or two of organization above anything that existed in Lincoln's time, that needs addressing first.

And the addressing of it is very severely hampered by the ideological narrowing I took as my starting point.

Immigration is a case in point.

I think the way to square a Lincolnian liberality with the national interest would be to secure the border and workplace so as to check any new flow [i.e. of illegals], then grant amnesty to illegal immigrants too embedded in their communities to leave the country.

All right, but *we already did all that in 1986.* We then discovered that powerful commercial and ideological forces can easily thwart the whole scheme, awarding Amnesty without any addition to security.

(In fairness I should say that Lowry also writes that: "We should stanch the flow of poorly educated immigrants, who compete for jobs with and suppress the wages of low-skilled workers." On the other *other* hand, he wants to welcome "skilled workers," who presumably he thinks—wrongly, says a mountain of evidence—do *not* compete for jobs with, and suppress the wages of, our own citizens.)

Personally I think Amnesty is a lousy idea; but whether it is or not, to pretend at this point that it can be dealt with in a trade for border and workplace security just sounds naïve. We are long past that possibility.

How to address those commercial and ideological forces, which are surely far more potent today than they were 27 years ago?

In particular, how to address them when they plainly have a firm, confident grip on both halves of the stage donkey?

These third- and fourth-level systemic problems, unknown to Abraham Lincoln's much simpler time, are the one we need to work on. And the working-on cannot be done from within the narrow confines of Establishment ideology—itself a product and a tool of those same obstructive forces. If we can't address our systemic problems, nor even—see Orwell up above—*talk* about them rationally, nothing can get fixed. No quantity of Establishment-compliant Whiggish pep talk will arrest our slide into political and cultural decay.

* * *

This article can be read online at http://www.vdare.com/articles/ lowry-on-lincoln-a-safe-whiggish-pep-talk-for-gop-loyalists-useless- on-the-real-issues

The Wonks' War Against the Sailer Strategy

September 12, 2013

Barack Obama's victory in the 2012 presidential election precipitated a running series of exchanges among election analysts centered on the topic: Can the Republican Party remain nationally competitive without making itself more appealing to minority voters?

Note that the differences of opinion—the interesting ones, at any rate—are coldly arithmetical, without moral content. It is possible to believe that Republicans *ought* to try harder to appeal to minorities, while yet believing that they can achieve electoral success without doing so.

That seems in fact to be the position of Sean Trende, a key participant in this War of the Wonks. On immigration reform, for example, Trende wrote this:

> From a "pure policy" standpoint, I find quite a bit to like in the basic "Gang of Eight" framework. But regardless of whether Republicans could or should back the bill, it simply isn't necessary for them to do so and remain a viable political force ["The Case of the Missing White Voters, Revisited," *Real Clear Politics*, June 21, 2013].

That is taken from the first essay in a four-part series Trende published in June-July this year. (Parts two, three, and four are titled, respectively, "Does GOP Have to Pass Immigration Reform?," "The GOP and Hispanics: What the Future Holds," and "Demographics and the GOP, Part IV.") That series in turn enlarges on a book Trende published earlier this year, *The Lost Majority*.

Trende argued, with numbers to back up the argument, that the biggest part of Mitt Romney's 2012 loss was due to "missing whites"—blue-collar northern and Midwestern whites who didn't show up at the polls in November.

(Note that "white," here and in what follows, refers to non-Hispanic whites.)

The GOP, said Trende, could build a fairly strong coalition by going after these downscale whites:

> It means abandoning some of its more pro-corporate stances. This GOP would have to be more "America first" on trade, immigration and foreign policy; less pro-Wall Street and big business in its rhetoric; more Main Street/populist on economics.

Various elements of the wonkerati rode into battle against Trende, brandishing their slide rules. Karl Rove, for example:

> To have prevailed over Mr. Obama in the electoral count, Mr. Romney would have had to carry 62.54% of white voters. That's a tall order, given that Ronald Reagan received 63% of the white vote in his 1984 victory. ["More White Votes Alone Won't Save the GOP," *Wall Street Journal*, June 26, 2013.]

(The slide rules there are purely symbolic. I may in fact be the last person in the Western world that knows how to use a slide rule. I actually have one here on my desk, a plastic model from ThinkGeek—handy enough, but not to be compared in *gravitas* with the fine old enameled wooden ones that used to be marketed to British schoolboys by a firm in Ulm, Germany—Albert Einstein's home town, we whispered to each other in awe.)

And then there was this from Alex Roarty at *National Journal*, a Washington, DC magazine for political professionals:

> If the GOP determines that its future lies with an all-out pursuit of whites, it might find an unwanted surprise. Some white voters, particularly young ones, won't align themselves with a party that can't attract support from Hispanics, African-

Americans, and Asians. To attract more white voters, the
GOP, ironically, might first need to attract more minorities.
["Why White Voters Will Flee a White-Only Party," August
1, 2013.]

Last week, *National Journal* published a longer, more detailed article along the same lines, but by a different analyst, Ronald Brownstein:

Can Republicans bet their future primarily on the notion that
the party can amass even bigger advantages with whites? The
answer depends on two distinct factors: turnout and vote-
share.... On both [these] fronts, a whites-first strategy would
face entrenched, structural challenges. For Republicans to increase the white share of the electorate in 2016 or beyond
would require them to reverse the virtually uninterrupted trajectory of the past three decades. ["Bad Bet: Why Republicans
Can't Win with Whites Alone," *National Journal*, September
5, 2013.]

That trajectory includes monotone trends in marriage, religion,
and education levels that are all (Brownstein argues) steadily eroding
the GOP base among whites. As white Americans become less married, less religious, and more educated—trends that show no signs of
reversing—the GOP is less appealing to them.

Brownstein makes a further point not much emphasized in prior
skirmishes: Barack Obama is unattractive to a lot of white voters, for
his past radicalism, and, yes, his color. A 2016 Democratic candidate
without that handicap might do *better* among whites—especially
among white women, if it was a woman. The bar for the GOP would
then be *higher* than in 2008 and 2012. In wonk-speak, Obama's share
of the white vote in 2012 (39 percent) may have been a *floor* for Democrats.

The wonkery here is, as you can see, very deep. For *VDARE.com* readers it is also deeply frustrating.

The central point of discussion here, the desirability of the GOP increasing its appeal to white voters, is the Sailer Strategy, which we have been airing, with full supporting numerical analyses, *since the 2000 election.*

We know that a prophet is without honor in his own country. But surely an occasional linked reference wouldn't hurt?

Note that, *contra* Ronald Brownstein's title, there are some *conceivable* circumstances in which Republicans *could* win with whites alone.

Whites were 72 percent of the electorate in 2012. On current demographic trends, that number will decline at roughly two percent per 4-year cycle. That gives us ten or a dozen cycles in which whites are a majority of the electorate—well past mid-century.

If whites were to vote for white GOP presidential candidates as tribally as blacks vote for a black Democrat, *with no additional votes from minorities at all*, the presidency would be decided by the white vote alone in all but the last of those cycles.

Even if whites nationwide just voted as tribally as white Mississippians did last November (89 percent for Romney), all but the last three of those cycles would be a lock.

Well, conceivable, perhaps, but neither thing will happen. Whites are too intensely engaged in their Cold Civil War—too much wrapped up in the pleasures of hating other whites—to unite as a tribe.

What *could* happen, what we should *wish* to happen, is a turn on the part of the GOP to economic populism, as recommended by Sean Trende, and more recently by my *VDARE.com* colleague James Kirkpatrick in his article on Colorado:

> Rather than serving as corporate lobbyists for the ultra-rich, the GOP should wage war on big money in politics and embrace a populist strategy against bankers, cheap labor, and offshoring.

A well-pitched populist appeal from an attractive candidate could reach parts that the current corporatist, big-donor-whipped GOP is not reaching. The fundamental issues are not hard to get across.

Those "Millennial" voters, for example, 76 percent of whom, *National Journal's* Alex Roarty tells us, "say immigrants make the country a stronger place," must include many seeking work in fields loaded up with H-1B immigrants.

How difficult would it be to explain to them that the H-1B worker is *indentured labor*, tied to a particular job with a particular employer? Why would a Millennial job-seeker not be indignant about that—indignant *not* at the immigrant, but at the employer who prefers indentured labor to free labor, at the immigration attorneys who game the system, and at the pols who enable it all?

We must hope for that turn on the GOP's part—and for that candidate.

It's worth noting, at a tangent from all the above, that even failing a populist turn, the GOP is by no means on the ropes. Republicans hold 30 of the 50 state governorships: 24 of them have a GOP-controlled state legislature to work with.

Certainly you should forget the apocalyptic remarks in some of that wonkery about the death of the Republican Party. Anglosphere political parties very rarely die: only under extraordinary historical circumstances, and never without some replacement party of similar orientation for voters to turn to.

The American Whig Party was chewed up by the slavery issue: Henry Clay Whigs became Abe Lincoln Republicans, at any rate in the North. The British Liberal Party succumbed to the post-WW1 radicalization of the working classes: Lloyd George Liberals (my grandfather) became Ramsay MacDonald Labour voters (my father).

For all the rancors of our public life, there are no such epochal issues dividing us at present. We shall be Democrats and Republicans for some time yet.

Sure, it's pleasant to dream of the present-day Republican Party, with its lickspittles, time-servers, and lunatics, being smashed to pieces. I see no prospect of this being done, though. The GOP will still be with us for many more presidential-election cycles. Conservatives can only hope to influence the party back *towards* a proper concern with the interests of ordinary citizens, *away from* the interests of foreigners and billionaire donors.

Only a tick above the probability of total Republican demise is that of a prolonged Democratic supremacy at the federal level. I have ruminated on this elsewhere:

> Such things happen. The most notable spell of party domination in a modern democracy was the so-called "Whig Supremacy" of 1714-1770 in Britain. (This time period actually encompassed one Tory Prime Minister, the Earl of Bute, 1762-3; but Bute was a brief aberration, the result of George the Third's first unsuccessful foray into parliamentary politics.) For 56 years—an entire adult lifetime!—the Whigs ran Britain and its overseas possessions, presenting themselves, very plausibly, as the party of peace, progress, prosperity and stability.

I wrote that in September 2000, though, in the context of predicting a Democratic victory in that year's presidential election. Oops. I have never since worried much about a one-party supremacy.

The Whig Supremacy of eighteenth-century Britain, a nation with a very limited electorate and deep dynastic and religious divisions, just does not map into modern mass politics. The U.S. presidency has even less to offer as examples of one-party supremacy, the Jeffersonians' 24-year run never equaled since, not even by post-Civil War Republicans or FDR Democrats.

A further tick above the probability of one-party supremacy is Noah Millman's "one-and-a-half-party state" at the federal level: long-term one-party supremacy in the legislature moderated by an opposition-party executive. This arrangement has been field-tested in Massachusetts, California, and New York City. But I can't see it "taking" at the federal level. The U.S. is too big and various.

The normal expectation for mass electoral politics is, as Sean Trende points out in his book, homeostasis. That is to say, as broad currents of mass opinion shift, party ideologies shift with them to maintain a rough 50-50 split for the major parties.

Absent historical cataclysms, parties do not die, or lie dormant for decades: they change shape in response to deeper cultural currents. The task for political activists and strong leaders is to influence the shape-changing.

I have not yet had a chance to read Alwyn Turner's latest book, *A Classless Society: Britain in the 1990s*, but I note this from the unsigned review in last week's *Economist*:

> The victory of Thatcherism had established a consensus for economic liberalism; social liberalism followed.... The changes in attitude of the 1990s had little to do with Britain's bewildered rulers.

What they *did* have to do with was the propagation, through the schools and the media, of 1960s radical egalitarianism in its mature form—what around here we call Cultural Marxism—with an assist from the final discrediting collapse of unsightly state Marxism.

We did not actually get the society without class of Turner's title; nor did we get a society without race, sex, sexual orientation, marital status, or religion.

What we got was widespread conversion to the belief that what Confucius called the Superior Man, the moral exemplar, should strive *not to notice* these things, not to use them in processing social information.

That is the cultural environment we have to work within.

It shouldn't be impossible. Moral convictions, even ones that defy reality—*there is no such thing as class, race, sex!*—should not leave their holders insensible to self-interest.

For example, even the most moral, i.e. moralistic, Millennial would be startled to learn that big firms are lobbying for more immigrants while laying off workers? ["Companies Lay Off Thousands, Then Demand Immigration Reform for New Labor," Byron York, *Washington Examiner*, September 11, 2013.]

Would be, that is, if anyone in the GOP dared to point it out to them.

* * *

This article can be read online at http://www.vdare.com/articles/ john-derbyshire-on-the-wonks-war-against-sailer-strategy

Scandinavian Reserve on Immigration Is Breaking Down

September 19, 2013

The performance of Norway's conservative/populist/classical-liberal Progress Party in that country's September 9th election caused much shrieking and swooning on the multicultural left.

One of the most piercing shrieks came from weirdly neckbearded sociologist Alf Gunvald Nilsen at the *Guardian* blog. ["Norway's Disturbing Lurch to the Right," September 10, 2013.]

Nilsen's column led off with a picture of fellow Norwegian Anders Breivik, perpetrator of the appalling July 2011 murders in Oslo and nearby Utøya Island. The connection here was that Breivik had belonged to the Progress Party in 1999-2007, resigning his membership because he found the party's line against multiculturalism insufficiently stern.

For an approximate equivalent, you can imagine *VDARE.com* running a story about Democrats doing well in the 2014 congressional midterm elections, the story prominently decorated with a picture of Washington Navy Yard killer Aaron Alexis, a liberal Democrat. (We promise not to.)

Mr. Nilsen's hyperventilating is even stranger in that the Progress Party's performance in this election was not very good, their representation in Norway's 169-seat parliament dropping from 41 seats to 29.

What disturbed Mr. Nilsen was rather the *overall* performance of the rightist parties, which together attained a wafer-thin parliamentary majority of 2 seats over the left-green coalition, which has been ruling since 2009 with a majority of 7. Some "lurch"!

Indeed, analysts discount the drop in support for Progress by noting that the Conservative Party, which did exceptionally well—from 30 seats to 48—has adopted some of the Progress Party's ideas, leading Progress supporters to some strategic vote-switching.

The rightist majority will only *be* a majority if Progress is fully included in government. Everyone assumes they will be. Progress helped prop up a center-right coalition in 2001-2005, but the coalition parties did not bring them in to decision-making. Now, with less of a fjord to be bridged between Conservative and Progress policy positions, there is no longer any reason for the mainstream Right to keep Progress at arm's length.

Progress is pretty much what *VDARE.com* urges our own Republican Party to be: low-tax, small-government, classical-liberal, culturally conservative, and immigration-restrictionist. It is led by 44-year-old, agreeably-Scandinavian-looking Siv Jensen (who, although a spinster, is *not* a strumpet: the headline *"Siv Jensen har stumpet røyken"* on that 2011 link translates as "Siv Jensen has quit smoking").

Even more encouraging to us, Progress went through a schism in the early 1990s over open-borders libertarianism. The Paulites eventually decamped and formed their own party, which soon withered on the vine.

Other good news from Norway: two years ago the Confederation of Norwegian Enterprise (NHO), a mainstream-conservative business lobby, came out *against* unskilled immigration, noting that (via Google Translate):

> Immigrants threaten the welfare state and [cost] too much. They work for a short time before they end up on welfare and [are] too little productive. ["NHO Will Have Fewer Immigrants," *ABC Nyheter*, May 10, 2011.]

There are some slight qualifications to be made there. The immigration being spoken of in the NHO report, which it is now quite respectable to oppose, is of Muslims and Africans—"asylum seekers," in the Euro-jargon of immigration. Immigration of Swedes, Poles, and Russians into Norway's small (5.1m) population is quite high and not objected to by anyone much, certainly not by business groups.

And traditional Scandinavian xenophilia remains intense among Norwegian elites. It was Norwegians, remember, who gave the Nobel Peace Prize to just-elected President Barack Obama for…well, let's be blunt: for being black. And much harm has already been done to Norway by mass Muslim immigration.

Still, a friend in Norway tells me that the configuration on the political right over there is "somewhat as if we had had intelligent Republican politicians in the U.S.A." We can dream.

Across the border in Sweden, meanwhile, the government has announced that it will give permanent resident status to all Syrian refugees who apply for asylum.

Since the United Nations has logged two million Syrians as being in a refugee status, with 4.25 million more displaced within the country, while Sweden's entire current population is only 9.5 million, this may qualify as the most insane public policy declaration in recent years, anywhere in the world—crazier even than George W. Bush's 2002 call for the trashing of rational credit standards in home-mortgage lending.

More astonishing yet, the government responsible for this bizarre decision is a center-right alliance dominated by the classic-liberal, low-tax, business-friendly Moderate Party. Though by no means *VDARE.com* conservatives, the alliance is well to the right of the Social Democrats who dominated Sweden in the post-WW2 decades and famously excited the disapproval of Dwight Eisenhower (antepenultimate paragraph here: http://pages.citebite.com/w2q1j0x3m2wux).

The nearest Swedish equivalent to Norway's Progress Party is the Sweden Democrats (by no means to be confused with the *Social* Democrats), who, since first entering the Swedish parliament in 2010, hold 20 of the 349 seats there.

The respectability gap between the Sweden Democrats and the governing center-right alliance is far wider than the Norwegian equivalent, though—more a gulf than a fjord. All the other parties in parliament have declared policies of non-cooperation with them.

Some of the difference springs from the personalities of the two nations. Until oil began to gush in the 1980s, Norway was a poor country of isolated, windswept settlements. Sweden was wealthier and more cosmopolitan—for a while in the modern era, even imperialist.

A rough comparison would be the Scots *versus* the English. Through poverty and hardship Norwegians became flintier, more cautious, and more sensible. Their great burst of prosperity this past 30 years has been well managed. The oil-rich Gulf Emirates have vending machines to dispense gold bars, and import Pakistanis and Filipinos to do all the work; oil-rich Norway has salted away their oil profits in a national fund for future generations.

The Sweden Democrats, like the British National Party, also had difficulty shaking off actual (as opposed to merely MSM-alleged) Neo-Nazi sympathizers brought along from its precursor parties. This was far less of an issue in Norway, which, unlike Sweden or Britain, was actually occupied by the Wehrmacht.

We should not, therefore, expect the Sweden Democrats to be a key component of their nation's government soon, as Norway's Progress Party has become. They are there in parliament, though, one more European political party speaking up for patriotic immigration reform.

Someone needs to do it. The ten days of rioting in immigrant areas of southern Sweden this May showed how far Sweden has gone down the path of national suicide. The city of Malmö is now a byword for Muslim violence and intolerance. The city's small number of Jews are particular targets:

> One who has had enough is Marcus Eilenberg, a 32-year-old Malmö-born lawyer, who is moving to Israel in April with his young family.
>
> "Malmö has really changed in the past year," he said. "I am optimistic by nature, but I have no faith in a future here for my children. There is definitely a threat….
>
> Mr. Eilenberg said he and his wife considered moving to Stockholm where Jews feel safer than in Malmö. "But we decided not to because in five years time I think it will be just as bad there," he said. ["Jews Leave Swedish City After Sharp Rise in Anti-Semitic Hate Crimes," *Daily Telegraph*, February 21, 2010.]

I wonder if it is too late for Mr. Eilenberg to have a word with Barbara Lerner Spectre?

Ann Corcoran at Refugee Resettlement Watch has a valuable paper trail, going back several years, on the consequences of mass immigration into Sweden. I refer readers to that link for further hair-raising details.

(And while I think of it, some archives from the long-defunct blog by Norwegian "Fjordman" survive on the internet in defiance of Peter Brimelow's glum prediction. Fjordman has also published a book, *Defeating Eurabia*.)

I shall have to leave the Danes, Finns, Icelanders, and Faroese for another time, but there is plainly a great deal to say about the future demographic prospects for Norway and Sweden. After years of conventional Scandinavian reserve, the peoples of those nations are at last beginning to say it.

* * *

This article can be read online at http://www.vdare.com/articles/ john-derbyshire-scandinavian-reserve-on-immigration-is-breaking-down

Black Privilege—A Ticket Off Death Row

October 10, 2013

We've been hearing a lot about "White Privilege" recently. My question: what about "Black Privilege"?

"White Privilege" is not as new an idea as you'd think: Ngram tracks it back to the 1950s, though the frequency curve didn't turn sharply upwards until the end of the 1980s. Possibly the concept of White Privilege escaped from the old U.S.S.R. as the Iron Curtain disintegrated. (Don't laugh; there probably is some connection there.)

I don't actually recall hearing about White Privilege much in the 1990s and 2000s. My impression is that it's only been pressed on us with real insistence the past year or two as the currently approved explanation for the persistently different statistical profiles of blacks *versus* nonblacks on measures of crime, scholastic attainment, poverty, bastardy, and so on. Ngram only goes to 2010, so I can't check.

These social-science explanations have a shelf life. They go stale—get dried-out and discolored, begin to curl at the edges. Fresh ones have to be brought in. So: out with "legacy of Jim Crow," in with "institutional racism." Then out with *that* and in with "White Privilege."

When the music stops, take the nearest chair.

It's tiresome, but we have to put up with it until, a decade or three from now, the social scientists are chased from the field by *real* scientists, and we actually understand the biological springs of human behavior, intelligence, and personality.

(If you have 12m 19s to spare, Jared Taylor addresses the topic of white privilege with his usual eloquence and wit in this video: http://www.amren.com/archives/videos/white-privilege)

But here is a different thing that happened in the late 1980s, the subsequent course of which can I think fairly be placed under a different heading—"black privilege."

136

On the chilly morning of Jan. 13, 1987, 67-year old Dr. William Chiapella and his 66-year old wife, Katherine, were found bound and gagged in their Downing Avenue home by their son. The couple had been stabbed multiple times and tortured before their death. ["Crittenden's Verdict in 1987 Chiapella Murders Overturned," *Action News Now* (Chico), October 5, 2013.]

That's Chico, California, a modestly prosperous little Whitopia—two percent black—eighty miles north of Sacramento, home to a campus of the state university.

(The TV people in that quote have the date wrong: the Chiapellas were *murdered* on the afternoon of the 13th, but their bodies were not found by their son until the 17th. They also have the Chiapellas' ages wrong: they were 68 and 67, according to the court transcripts. You'd be surprised how hard it is to find news reports whose details agree with official records. The *Sacramento Bee* misspells the county D.A.'s name: it's Ramsey, not Ramsay. Way to go, journo schools!)

Steven Edward Crittenden, a 19-year-old "student-athlete" at the Chico campus, was arrested for the crime on January 21st 1987 and subsequently brought to trial. Evidence presented to the court included:

- Crittenden had done yard work for the Chiapellas the previous fall after responding to an advertisement they placed on the college job board.

- He had money problems and was behind with the rent for his off-campus apartment. On January 11th, two days before the murder, he assured his landlord he'd be able to pay what he owed by the 14th.

- On the morning of the 13th Crittenden's roommate noticed that a knife he owned was missing. Crittenden said he had borrowed it to fix his stereo and would return it.

- A neighbor identified the unusually tall (6 ft. 4 in.) Crittenden as a man he had seen on the Chiapellas' property the afternoon of the murder.

- On January 14th Crittenden cashed a check for $3,000 made out to him by Mrs. Chiapella and dated the previous day.

- Both the Chiapellas were badly beaten before being stabbed to death. Mr. Chiapella had been tortured.

- One of Mrs. Chiapella's stab wounds was consistent with the roommate's missing knife (which Crittenden returned on the 14th).

- The cloth used to bind and gag the Chiapellas had the same pattern as that of sheets and matching pillowcases belonging to Crittenden's apartment when he moved in. When police searched the apartment they found the sheets but not the pillowcases.

- Also in Crittenden's apartment, police found a pair of tennis shoes matching a bloody print found in the Chiapellas' house.

- Crittenden's thumbprint was found on an ATM slip in the Chiapellas' study.

- Asked about his movements on the afternoon of the 13th, Crittenden first told police he had been "partying." Then he changed his story, saying he had gone to his gym where he had met a basketball coach and two other persons. But the coach and one of the other persons testified they had not seen Crittenden since January 7th.

- Crittenden claimed that Mrs. Chiapella had been paying him for sex since the previous August. The $3,000 January 13th check was, he said, in payment for a sex act performed in Room 96 of a local motel on January 9th. There is no record of either Crittenden or Mrs. Chiapella being at the motel that day, and it has no Room 96.

Crittenden was found guilty in April 1989 on two counts of first-degree murder. After the following penalty phase of the trial, the jury deliberated for 17 hours over four days, then handed down a death sentence.

Both the conviction and the penalty were upheld by the California Supreme Court in 1994. Crittenden has spent the last 24 years on San Quentin's Death Row.

But he may soon be out. On September 30th U.S. District Judge Kimberly J. Mueller, an Obama appointee, threw out Crittenden's conviction. She gave state law enforcement authorities 60 days to either release Crittenden from prison or file new charges against him preparatory to a retrial.

Obviously, trying Crittenden again 26 years after the event is going to present serious evidentiary problems. There is an excellent chance that Crittenden is off the hook.

Why did Judge Mueller overturn his conviction? Well, Crittenden is black. In the 50-person jury pool, there was only one black. The trial prosecutor, Gerald E. Flanagan, used one of his 26 peremptory strikes to dismiss that person because she had negative feelings about the death penalty.

No, no, wrote Judge Mueller, that was not the *true* reason that Flanagan dismissed the lady. She wrote:

> At the time of Flanagan's rating of jurors after voir dire and the time of his actually striking [the juror], Flanagan was motivated, consciously or unconsciously, in substantial part by race. ["Judge Overturns Former Prep Gridiron Star's Death-Penalty Conviction," Fairfield-Suisun (Calif.) *Daily Republic*, October 9, 2013.]

In evidence of Prosecutor Flanagan's conscious-or-unconscious racism, Judge Mueller adduced the following:

- On the jury selection checklist, Flanagan gave the black juror a low score while giving another death penalty opponent a higher score.

- Flanagan used the term "gas chamber" almost only with the black potential juror. Mueller described the term as a "charged descriptor." (I haven't been able to discover what "almost only" means in this report.)

- Flanagan had dismissed a black person during jury selection in a previous trial.

Now, it is possible that this kind of exquisite punctiliousness, this judicial divining of a prosecutor's inner motivations 24 years after the event on dust motes of circumstantial evidence, it is *possible* that somewhere in the legal annals of our republic similar efforts have been put forth on behalf of a nonblack defendant whose conviction is suspected, on equally microscopic grounds, to have been marred by some bias other than hostility to blacks.

It may be that a nonblack person has been the recipient of judicial largesse on this extravagant scale. I don't know; I have no access to the nation's legal databases. Perhaps someone who does, can point out a case to me.

Until they do, I am going to call this "black privilege."

And I am then going to predict that if we get many more judges like Kimberly J. Mueller on the federal bench, conviction of any black person for anything at all will soon be impossible.

* * *

This article can be read online at http://www.vdare.com/articles/ john-derbyshire-on-black-privilege-a-ticket-off-death-row

Worse Than America! Lampedusa and European Elite's Suicidal Insouciance

October 31, 2013

In the space of a few weeks there, two news stories came along with an obvious connection between them. Outside the sphere of Dissident Right websites, however, the connection was not made. Respectable persons all over the Western world are now well-schooled in what Orwell called "crimestop"—the power of *not thinking* forbidden thoughts.

- ***Story Number One:***

...was the release in mid-June of the U.N. World Population Prospects report. The population projections for Africa were particularly striking. The U.N. estimates that the population of Niger, for example, will increase from today's 18 million to 204 million by the end of the century—more than present-day Brazil. The former Belgian Congo will have 262 million, more than today's Russia and Mexico combined.

Population scares are of course nothing new. Biologist Paul Ehrlich made our flesh creep with his book *The Population Bomb* 45 years ago, and Dr. Malthus was working the field 170 years before that.

The U.N. demographers did not set out to write a best-selling book, though, nor to make philosophical points about human nature, only to project present trends in fertility and mortality into the next few decades, with different—though all reasonable—assumptions yielding low, medium, and high variants for the resulting numbers. Table S.2 in their report, from which I took the data in the second paragraph above, uses the medium variant. This is simple numerical work.

And yes, there have been some impressive drops in fertility over recent decades, especially in the Islamic world. Table S.11 shows nations with the largest and smallest changes in fertility between the late 70s and the late 00s. The average Iranian woman went from producing 6.28 children in her lifetime to 1.89. On the other hand, fertility in Somalia *increased* in those 30 years from 7.00 to 7.10 children per woman.

Comparing their results with those of the previous report of two years ago, the U.N. authors say:

> In the new revision, the estimated total fertility rate (TFR) for 2005-2010 has increased in several countries, including by more than 5 per cent in 15 high-fertility countries from sub-Saharan Africa. *In some cases, the actual level of fertility appears to have risen in recent years*; in other cases, the previous estimate was too low. [*World Population Prospects, The 2012 Revision: Key Findings and Advance Tables*, U.N. Department of Economic and Social Affairs, Population Division, June 2013; my italics.]

- *Story Number Two:*

…was the October 3rd catastrophe off the Italian island of Lampedusa, when more than 300 people from sub-Saharan Africa drowned when the boat they were packed into capsized. Most of the victims were from Eritrea and Somalia, though there seem to have been some West Africans among the dead, too.

The Africans were of course trying to get to Europe as "refugees" or "asylum seekers," although a typical Lampedusa boatload seems to consist of healthy, well-fed-looking young men (and the occasional woman), while the coyote fee, which can run to several thousand dollars, is far beyond the financial resources of most in the sending countries. Just the boat trip from the Libyan port of Tripoli costs $1,200, and Tripoli is 3,000 miles from Somalia.

The cool numeracy of the U.N. population report generated a scattering of news stories, then disappeared. Numbers—who cares about numbers? The Lampedusa disaster, with its immediate human-interest content, proved more enduring.

The Italians, even though they are in the forefront of the issue, seem remarkably clueless about the larger implications of what is happening—or perhaps exceptionally proficient at crimestop. Enrico Letta, Italy's fool of a Prime Minister, seems to have promised *state funerals* to the victims, and:

> Letta said he considered it a disgrace that survivors of the disaster had automatically been placed under investigation thanks to the Italian law against clandestine migration, even if they would likely be eligible for asylum. ["Lampedusa Shipwreck: Italy to Hold State Funeral for Drowned Migrants," Tom Kington, *The Guardian*, October 9, 2013.]

Signor Letta seems later to have backed off from the state funerals, but he did grant Italian citizenship to the dead. Whether that grant extends to the wives and children of the deceased (or those who may plausibly claim to be such) back in the Horn of Africa, I haven't been able to discover. But Letta seems to be doing his best to *encourage* the flow off illegal immigrants from Africa into Europe.

Among the cultural spin-offs from the Lampedusa affair was a radio program broadcast by Britain's BBC on October 16th.

The program was one episode of a weekly series with overall title *The Moral Maze*. The format is for a panel of four program regulars, under the direction of a moderator, to interrogate invited expert "witnesses" on some topic with a moral dimension: abortion, business ethics, pornography, "Is Wagner's music morally tainted by his anti-Semitism?" and so on.

The October 16th episode of *The Moral Maze* had "migration" as its topic, with particular reference to the Lampedusa disaster.

(I note in passing here the preference on the part of leftists and open-borders propagandists—the BBC is heavily loaded with both—for the word "migration" over "immigration." "Migration" has a reassuring look of *equivalence* about it, as if the flows are multidirectional. *Some Somalis want to settle in Europe; some Europeans want to settle in Somalia; what's the problem?* There is a whole column to be written about these terminological sleights of hand, but I'll leave it for another time.)

The BBC doesn't publish transcripts of the program—or if it does, I couldn't find one—so I made a transcript myself and posted it here: http://www.johnderbyshire.com/Opinions/NationalQuestion/moralmaze.html. It includes full instructions for downloading or listening to the original program.

The program commences with a brief, neutral description of the week's topic by the moderator. Then each of the panel members in turn states his own opening position on the topic in a hundred words or less.

Here we were deep in BBC-land. There were four panelists: a lifetime inhabitant of Leftish policy think tanks, a Left-libertarian harpy who was formerly a stalwart of Britain's Revolutionary Communist Party, an Anglican priest who was awarded the Stonewall Hero of the Year award in 2012 for contributions to homosexuality, and an *Economist* editor. For us old *Daily Telegraph* readers, the shade of the late Michael Wharton hovered over the proceedings.

Two of these four, the harpy and the priest, stated frank open-borders positions. The harpy said that "the immigrant is an ideal moral figure"; the priest quoted Emma Lazarus with gusto.

The other two averred degrees of enthusiasm ("I think migration has benefited Britain" and "I take a relatively generous view of immigration") but with some cautious qualifications.

That's how far the thing was tilted to the Open-Borders position: an *Economist* editor was on the restrictionist side!

The program's four "witnesses" were very little better.

Moderator: Our first witness is Dr. Phillip Cole, who's Senior Lecturer in Politics and International Relations at the University of the West of England, written extensively on migration, including *Debating the Ethics of Immigration: Is There a Right to Exclude?* Er, is there?

Cole: No. There isn't a right to exclude.

Moderator: So in your view, should all borders be wide open?

Cole: Yes, they should.

Hoo-ee. The leftish-wonk panelist scored the best points from Dr. Cole:

> Can I just probe this incredibly pure position that you have about Open Borders, with a bit of kind of *reductio ad absurdum*? The Sentinelese tribe of the Andaman Islands, they're one of the most remote tribes in the world, and the international community recognizes that we should leave them alone, because they respond very badly to outsiders. Would you be completely laid back if a thousand twentysomething Westerners decided to land on the Andaman Islands tomorrow because they just fancied, you know, getting away from things?

Journalist Ed West, author of *The Diversity Illusion: What We Got Wrong About Immigration & How to Set It Right* (noticed on *VDARE.com* back in April) was the next "witness" up. But he got tangled in theology with the priest and in political philosophy with the harpy, to no enlightening purpose.

Speaking as a fellow sufferer from chronic *esprit d'escalier*, I offer Ed my sympathy.

Third "witness" was an Italian chap from the Institute for Research into Superdiversity. You didn't know there was such an institute, did you? Neither did I. In fact, dwelling as I do in reactionary darkness, I didn't even know there was such a *thing* as superdiversity until I looked up these participants' bios. You learn something every day.

The Italian superdiversicrat unfortunately had trouble making sense, not entirely because of his imperfect command of English. The only thing I could figure out was that he did *not* want the African illegals sent back to Africa.

The sturdiest opposition to the Open-Borders crowd came from author Harriet Sergeant, who does social research at a Thatcherite think tank. She was the only one of the eight participants to speak up at length for the historic native populations of Europe. After the priest had noted gaily that immigration is good because it benefits immigrants she riposted:

> The people who have *not* benefited are the poor.... Because their schools are overcrowded, the hospitals are overcrowded, they can't get housing.... So I think, actually, I actually have a moral problem with, with sort of middle-class people sitting round discussing, saying how wonderful immigration is, when actually for us, it is all to the good.

Even Ms. Sergeant, though, made it clear that she believes mass immigration has an upside. Vibrancy! Those ethnic restaurants!

> *Priest*: I love London...London's a town that immigration has built, isn't it?
>
> *Ms. Sergeant*: I couldn't agree more. I, I don't like to admit this, but I grew up in London during the seventies, when we had very little immigration, and it was a deeply dreary city, frankly. So I agree with you enormously.

As it happens, I lived in London in the seventies too, when it was still majority white British, which is no longer the case. People *shunned* the "vibrant" areas. A local joke at the time went: *Q*—How can we reduce street crime in London? *A*—shut down the Victoria Line. (The Victoria Line of the London subway system had just been extended to Brixton, a black area.)

I found 1970s London a lively place full of interesting people of all classes. "Deeply dreary"? Ms. Sergeant didn't get out much.

For a window into the suicidal insouciance of the European elites, this little 43-minute cultural snippet is hard to beat. You can download it from the BBC website or read my transcript. Harriet Sergeant's gestures to the native working class and Ed West's attempt to distinguish law from morality both aside, the overall atmosphere is thick with denial, ignorance, ethnomasochism, xenophilia, and smug moral universalism.

That homosexual priest:

> Our moral responsibility is always to this person who is more *other* than us, rather than *same* as us.

I wonder if the speaker believes he has more moral responsibility to heterosexuals than to homosexuals? Orwell came to mind again: "A Humanitarian is always a hypocrite."

American listeners can take some comfort from the fact, clearly on display here, that the cultural death-wish has a firmer grip on the other side of the Atlantic than it yet has here. There is a stifled, constipated quality about the *Moral Maze* discussion that you don't find here, not even—well, not to the same degree—on NPR, which is our closest equivalent to the BBC. The Europeans are far gone into the night, much further than us.

In Britain, anti-racism is at levels of clinical hysteria. A white person can be ostracized over there for using the word "colored." Attempts at mild racial humor will get you investigated by the police. An accusation of racism is so potent, people will hesitate and deliberate earnestly before inflicting it on their worst political enemies. Harmless citizens accused of the dread heresy squeal their innocence pathetically: "But I'm not racist!"

Hence the walking-on-eggshells quality of some of the exchanges.

Moderator: I don't know what you thought, Claire, but [I was] slightly wary when, um, when Dr. Cole said, when taxed I think by Anne, er, what about democracy, what about the opinions of the, if you like, the existing resident population, er, he kind of said, um, he, he seemed to imply that people who, who took the opposite point of view to him were inherently unreasonable.

Harpy: Er, as xenophobic, or even hinting at racism....

Moderator: Er, he didn't, he didn't say that. I mean, he, he, er....

Harpy: No, but I, but I, no, but I'm say....

Here is a suggestion for the BBC program producers: We here at *VDARE.com* have been toiling in the vineyards of immigration policy for well over a decade now. We know the data, the history, and the arguments, and we're schooled in a more open environment of debate, an environment less in thrall to the rigid dogmas of superdiversity and less cowed by the heresy-sniffers. Some of us, when accused of being "racist," have been known to smile benignly and say: "Yes. What's it to ya?"

So next time you want to do a thumb-sucker program on this topic, why not bring in the New World to redress the balance of the Old?

Why not invite one of *us* on your program?

* * *

This article can be read online at http://www.vdare.com/articles/ john-derbyshire-worse-than-america-lampedusa-and-european-elite-s-suicidal-insouciance

On Abolitionist Porn and Antebellum Economics

November 21, 2013

It seems I've picked up an interest in the Civil War just as America is undergoing a revival of Abolitionist Porn. That, at any rate, is what I take this much-talked-of new movie *12 Years a Slave* to be.

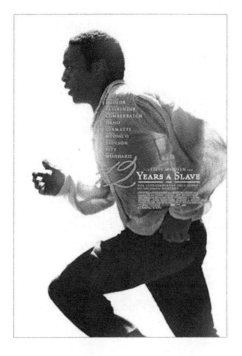

No, I haven't seen the thing, but I've read reviews. Also I've seen (and reviewed) a specimen of the allied genre: Civil Rights Porn.

And I've no doubt there *was* such a thing as Abolitionist Porn. It would have been surprising if there wasn't. Whenever there's a deep and long-standing difference between two sets of social principles, a genre of lurid tales will come up in one camp, denigrating the other.

For example: Back when England was bumptiously Protestant, there was Anti-Catholic Porn: Try the lip-smacking description of two Catholic clerics—a monk and a bishop—being hanged in Chapter 26 of Charles Kingsley's *Westward Ho!*

(When I mentioned this to a friend, he told me that Anti-*Mormon* Porn was popular for some decades around 1900, and urged me to read the 1912 Zane Grey Western classic *Riders of the Purple Sage*. I haven't yet, but it's on my list.)

So I've no doubt that antebellum Yankees enjoyed having their flesh made to creep by stories of the dreadful goings-on in Southern plantations.

There was at least enough of this kind of thing for Southerners to poke fun at it. Here is *Gone with the Wind's* Scarlett O'Hara making business calls on occupying Yankees in Reconstruction Atlanta:

> Accepting *Uncle Tom's Cabin* as revelation second only to the Bible, the Yankee women all wanted to know about the blood-hounds which every Southerner kept to track down runaway slaves. And they never believed her when she told them she had only seen one bloodhound in all her life.... They wanted to know about the dreadful branding irons which planters used to mark the faces of their slaves...and they evidenced what Scarlett felt was a very nasty and ill-bred interest in slave con-cubinage. [*Gone with the Wind*, Chapter 38.]

Reading that, and knowing something of the author's background, I thought: Well, I bet there *were* bloodhounds; but I also bet there were young plantation women who had seen only one.

Some googling on the *Slave Narratives* confirms the first, at any rate. The *Slave Narratives* are recorded reminiscences from ex-slaves, gathered by the Federal Writers' Project in 1936-38. The speaker here was born "around 1852":

> Mars George fed an' clo'esed well an' was kin' to his slaves, but once in a while one would git onruly an' have to be pun-ished. De worse I ever seen one whupped was a slave man dat had slipped off an' hid out in de woods to git out of wuk. Dey chased him wid blood hounds, an' when dey did fin' him dey

tied him to a tree, stroppin' him 'round an' 'round. Dey sho' did gib him a lashin'. [*Mississippi Slave Narratives*, Harriet Walker.]

As that extract illustrates, though, the *Slave Narratives* also remind us how remarkably often ex-slaves spoke well of their masters.

Plainly there was more to American race slavery that white masters brutalizing resentful Negroes. How much more, though? What was slavery actually *like?*

Trying to get to grips with this, I found it easiest to divide up the topic the way Caesar divided Gaul, into three parts:

- Slavery as a condition.

- American slave society as a way of life.

- The position of blacks in America's first century.

Of slavery as a condition—the ownership of human beings—the first thing to be said is that any person of feeling and imagination has to think it wrong, on the Golden Rule principle. The liberty to work out your own destiny, by your own volition, is a sweet thing, as the Spartans told the Persian. I wouldn't deprive anyone of it.

That said, some historical imagination is in order. People are born, raised, educated, and find themselves in a certain kind of society to which those around them are all accustomed. American slave society *was* a way of life; a settled way that most people took for granted, as most people will anywhere.

There were aspects of life resembling slavery in the communist China where I lived, 1982-3. People had no liberty to find their own employment. You were "assigned" to a "unit." If unhappy there, it was a devil of a job to get re-assigned.

Families broken up? One of my Chinese colleagues lived alone because his wife was "assigned" to a distant province. He only saw her once a year.

The guy drank a lot.

Yet while there was much grumbling, and some scattered seething rebelliousness, most Chinese got along with the system. A lot of people were very happy with it. You didn't have to think much, or take much responsibility. And that suits many of us just fine.

You glimpse something similar in the *Slave Narratives*:

> Lak all de fool N——s o' dat time I was right smart bit by de freedom bug for awhile. It sounded pow'ful nice to be tol': "You don't have to chop cotton no more. You can th'ow dat hoe down an' go fishin' whensoever de notion strikes you. An' you can roam 'roun' at night a' court gals jus' as late as you please. Aint no marster gwine a-say to you, 'Charlie, you's got to be back when de clock strikes nine.'"
>
> I was fool 'nough to b'lieve all dat kin' o' stuff. But to tell de hones' truf, mos' o' us didn' know ourse'fs no better off. Freedom meant us could leave where us'd been born an' bred, but it meant, too, dat us had to scratch for us ownse'fs. Dem what lef' de old plantation seamed so all fired glad to git back dat I made up my min' to stay put. I stayed right wid my white folks as long as I could. [*Mississippi Slave Narratives*, Charlie Davenport.]

Slavery is more irksome to some than to others; and freedom can be irksome, too. Personally, I'd be a terrible slave—too ornery. I know people, though—and I'm talking about white people—who I quietly suspect would be happy in slavery.

To get some understanding of American slave society as a way of life, you have to go to the academic studies, of which of course there have been a great number.

I can't claim to have done more than scratch the surface here. Eugene Genovese's *Roll, Jordan Roll* seems to me a good narrative survey, with plenty of quotations and diary extracts from people of the time.

Genovese was a Marxist when he wrote the book, but it only shows in patches here and there. His familiarity with Hegel, one of Marx's inspirations, is actually quite illuminating, for example in the inversion of the master-servant relationship:

> A slaveholding Confederate soldier who had to send his body servant home insisted upon his early return. "He is a great darky—worth his weight in gold even in these hard times," he glowed, explaining. "He can tell you what things I principally need & more fully than I can write—he knows more about it anyway than I do, knows more about what I have and what I need—he attends to it all."

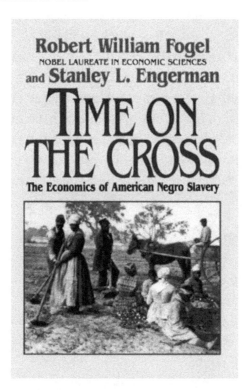

For a more data-rich account, Fogel and Engerman's *Time on the Cross* is fascinating, full of counterintuitive insights.

Life expectancy? After crunching the numbers:

U.S. slaves had much longer life expectations than free urban industrial workers in both the United States and Europe.

We're talking about a period, remember, when life was very wretched for a great many free men: the period of Mayhew's *London Labour and the London Poor*, and of Hugo's *Les Misérables*.

And we all know about white plantation overseers; but *black* overseers? Oh, yeah: After crunching more numbers from census data and plantation records:

> The conclusion indicated by these findings is startling: On a majority of the large plantations, the top nonownership management was black.

That's on the way to arguing that black plantation labor was *better*—more skillful, more productive—than previous scholars had thought. Fogel and Engerman want to disprove the "false stereotypes of [black] incompetence" that, they say, were imposed on blacks for more than a century.

These good intentions notwithstanding, I am told (by Bob Weissberg, who knows this territory well) that *Time on the Cross* is in serious disfavor with the current generation of social scientists for painting too nuanced a picture of Southern slave society.

It's not hard to see why. Take the matter of what Scarlett O'Hara referred to as "slave concubinage." Where *did* all those mulattoes come from, if not from plantation owners and white overseers having their way with helpless Negro slave women?

Genovese quotes Mary Chesnut's diaries on this topic:

> Like the patriarchs of old, our men live all in one house with their wives and their concubines; and the mulattoes one sees in every family partly resemble the white children. Any lady is ready to tell you who is the father of all the mulatto children in

everybody's household but her own. Those, she seems to think, drop from the clouds.

Northerners who visited the South came to similar conclusions.

Fogel and Engerman, however, go to the numbers:

> It is not the eyesight of these travelers to the South which is questionable, but their statistical sense. For mulattoes were not distributed evenly through the Negro population. They were concentrated in the cities and especially among freedmen.... The share of Negro children fathered by whites on slave plantations probably averaged between 1 and 2 percent.

Plantation records and diaries show that overseers were sternly warned against fraternizing with slave women, and were generally dismissed if they did so, as their adventures "could undermine the discipline that planters so assiduously strove to attain."

Venturing into *very* seriously un-PC territory, Fogel and Engerman argue that Southern white men anyway did not desire black women, an aversion the authors put down to "racism." They support this with some data from Nashville:

> The 1860 census showed that just 4.3 percent of the prostitutes in that city were Negroes, although a fifth of the population of Nashville was Negro. Moreover, all of the Negro prostitutes were free and light-skinned.... White men who desired illicit sex had a strong preference for white women.

Again, the authors are on their way here to a refutation of the stereotype of black promiscuity. Fogel and Engerman really meant well.

It has done them no good, of course: their fascinating book is down there with *The Bell Curve* in liberal esteem. Human kind cannot bear very much reality.

For the third of my three divisions of Gaul, the position of blacks in America's first century, I've been getting some insights from Gene Dattel's 2009 excellent book *Cotton and Race in the Making of America*.

Dattel's main focus is on the sheer size and importance of the cotton business to *both North and South*. Did you know that cotton was America's leading export from 1803 to 1937?

> Northerners played a leading role in the cotton economy of the South and its accompanying racial disaster. Racial animosity and hypocrisy have been an underappreciated but fundamental aspect of the white North, both before and after the Civil War.

As a chronicler of racial hypocrisy, Dattel is unsparing. White Northerners, *including abolitionists*, did not want free blacks living among them, and invested much energy in keeping blacks in the South picking cotton while white immigrants poured in to the North and West. Remember that the family of Eliza, in *Uncle Tom's Cabin,* having freed themselves, emigrate to Liberia at last.

Dattel writes:

> We forget that anti-slavery for the most part also meant anti-black. White Americans have decoupled the horrors of slavery from the condition of free blacks. In a fit of national self-congratulation, Americans have applauded emancipation and relapsed into historical amnesia with respect to the condition of blacks in the North.

If you're looking for the roots of present-day liberal hypocrisy on race, here they are.

Civil rights? Dattel writes:

> [Reconstruction-era] Republican congressman Samuel W. Moulton of Illinois supported civil rights legislation *to contain*

freedmen in the South. He was quite explicit: "Whenever the colored man is completely and fully protected in the southern states he will never visit Illinois, and he will never visit Indiana, and every northern state will be depopulated of colored people as will be Canada." [My italics.]

I'm normally skeptical of economistic explanations for historical events. But Dattel is convincing that the financial power of cotton, combined with the natural racial antipathy between white and black, drove U.S. history for almost a century and a half, through the slave era and beyond.

There's much to learn here, and I'll gratefully take book recommendations from readers, email me at olimu@johnderbyshire.com.

In the matter of slavery, though, I already feel sure that the shallow good North, bad South simplicities of Abolitionist Porn and popular perception bear little relation to the thorny tangles of reality.

* * *

This article can be read online at http://www.vdare.com/articles/ john-derbyshire-on-abolitionist-porn-and-antebellum-economics

Race-Whipped Conservatives
and the Stigma of "Racism"—
Or: Robert VerBruggen Loves Big Brother!

December 19, 2013

Robert VerBruggen's piece "The Stigma of Racism" at *RealClear-Policy.com* has been widely noted on the race-realist websites, mainly for purposes of mockery.

The topic of the piece is a study conducted by a Harvard professor on people's willingness to admit having noticed race. The setup for the study is:

- A screen showing twelve faces, six white and six black.

- Volunteer X, who silently selects one face from the twelve.

- Volunteer Y, who has to discover which face X selected by asking X a series of yes-no questions.

By asking "Is the person black?" Y could eliminate half the faces right away. However, most Ys did not ask this question, nor mention race at all, *especially* when X was black.

Yet that majority of Ys who did not mention race were *more likely* to be perceived as racist by X—more likely, that is, than the minority who did mention race. ["The Costs of Racial 'Color Blindness'," Michael I. Norton and Evan P. Apfelbaum, *Harvard Business Review,* July-August 2013.]

So far, so good, although nothing very surprising. As VerBruggen says:

> [Many whites] place so much importance on demonstrating that black people don't make them nervous that black people make them nervous.

But he then goes on to tell us that this is a jolly good thing:

> Going from Jim Crow to white people who refuse to utter the words "Is the person black?"—often categorically, but frequently in deference to a nearby person of color [*sic*]—in 50 years is a remarkable accomplishment for the civil-rights movement, both as a social force and as a driver of government policy.

As I said, the piece drew some mocking responses. The *Countenance Blog* was particularly scathing:

> So, a knave who…praises as "a remarkable accomplishment for the civil rights movement" the fact that we have gone "from Jim Crow to white people refusing to utter the words" is all of a sudden upset when white people self-censor and engage in informal affirmative action.

AmRen posted an edited version of VerBruggen's piece which generated a long comment thread. Several commenters stated the obvious thing: that the "remarkable accomplishment for the civil rights movement" that VerBruggen rhapsodizes over consists in having instilled justified fear in nonblacks—the fear that they will lose their jobs if they venture outside the narrow bounds of approved discourse by so much as a millimeter.

By that criterion, the greatest social "accomplishments" of the 20th century were those of Stalin, Mao Tse-tung, Kim Il Sung, and Pol Pot.

Chuck at *glpiggy.net* noted the piece but eschewed mockery, only adding an anecdote of his own.

> I was in 4th grade—9 or 10 years old. I was asked to explain latitude, as in the east-west running lines on a map or globe. I tiptoed around the best explanation I'd heard up to that point which was that latitude rhymes with fatitude and the latitude lines at the equator on a map look like the waist line of a fat person. But I avoided saying 'fat' because there were some chubby kids in my class. So I stammered around and made up some other explanation.

It's a nice anecdote, but not really relevant. Pointing out a fat person's fatness might hurt his feelings, a thing polite people are naturally reluctant to do.

I have childhood memories—no doubt we all do—of being scolded by parents for staring at people who were hunchbacked, birthmarked, one-armed, or physically abnormal in some other way. "It's not *polite*. He can't *help* it...."

I can't see how this relates to blackness, though. A hunched back, a birthmark, or a missing arm are all pitiable conditions. So, at a slight stretch, is obesity. What's pitiable about being black?

I'm assuming that Robert VerBruggen has left *National Review*, where we used to meet around the editorial table on alternate Mondays. (He hasn't posted there since June, and his byline says he's *"editor of RealClearPolicy."*) I have retained no very strong memory of him, but that's no reflection on his character. He was a rather quiet and unassuming person, and my memory isn't very good.

I do vaguely recall thinking that VerBruggen was sound on Second Amendment issues, but unsound—from the point of view of a traditionalist conservative—on others. A couple of data points:

- At one editorial meeting he waxed indignant about "bullying" in schools, an issue then beginning to be promoted by the Cultural-Marxist left. I said that the "bullying" fuss was cover for a campaign by homosexualists to normalize buggery among high-schoolers.

VerBruggen was profoundly shocked. Plainly my dart had landed well wide of his personal Overton Window. I can't remember what he said, but I remember the tone of muted outrage in which he said it. The tone expressed something like: *I have never in my life heard anyone say anything so shockingly disgraceful.*

- It was he that was editor for my February 2011 diary at *National Review Online.* The diary as submitted included a segment on the scuppering of that year's American Renaissance conference by the Mayor pro tem of Charlotte, North Carolina.

Knowing how race-whipped *National Review* is, I strove to present the issue in terms that would be acceptable to them, as a matter of free speech.

My efforts were in vain. When the diary appeared on NRO's website, that segment had been excised.

Whether VerBruggen dropped the segment on his own initiative, or whether he sought a ruling from further up the NRO chain of command, I don't know.

Reading VerBruggen's piece, and the race-realist responses to it, my first thought was that the gulf here is generational. VerBruggen (pictured next page) is a young fellow—hardly more than thirty, I would guess. If that's right, his key educational experiences were in the 1990s, when Cultural Marxism was settling on the U.S. educational system like poisonous ash from a volcanic eruption.

My own kids, born 1993 and 1995, were only a few years behind that, and I saw how intensely they were schooled *to pretend not to notice* race.

I recall one dinner-time conversation when my daughter was in high school. Mrs. Derbyshire mentioned some family we knew very slightly—call them the Blanks—whose son had been accepted into Columbia University.

Me: "Good for him. The Blanks…. They're Jewish, aren't they?"

My daughter: "*Da-ad!* Really! You're *terrible!*"

I can't honestly remember whether she left the table in disgust, but she was in a mood to. You're not supposed to *notice*.

To a person of my generation and background, such things are interesting features of the social landscape, with no particular emotional coloring. They're Jewish.... He's black.... She's a lesbian.... That kid's adopted.... Sam should really lose some weight....

These are things we notice about persons, and bring up in conversation, *without any intent to commit violence against those persons, nor even to strip them of their civil rights!*

To most people of less than middle age, however, there is something morally suspect about noticing any person's racial, sexual, ancestral, or physical characteristics other than the most innocuous. The minefield begins somewhere not far beyond: "He's pretty tall."

These exquisite sensitivities seeped down from the media and educational systems across the closing decades of the last century. Twenty years ago they had still not infected many ordinary citizens. I told the following story in Chapter 6 of my worldwide bestseller *We Are Doomed*:

> I came home from work on the Long Island Railroad one day in December, 1993. My train was right behind the one in which Colin Ferguson went berserk and shot 25 people. We were held up for a long time, and there were no cell phones. My poor wife was at home, watching news of the shooting on TV. For all she knew, I might have been among the dead. Kind neighbors came round to keep her company. Telling me about it afterwards, she remarked: "They kept saying the same thing: 'It must be a black guy. If it was a white guy, they would have told us....'"

I don't think so many people would say nowadays what my neighbors said in 1993. The indoctrination is now more nearly complete. We love Big Brother.

Robert VerBruggen sure does.

> The campaign to stigmatize anti-black racism—the most corrosive force in this country's history—has been remarkably successful. In fact, while we love to talk about this or that as

"the last acceptable prejudice," it would be more accurate to say that racism and sexism are the only prejudices that are thoroughly unacceptable.

The definitions of "racism" and "sexism" VerBruggen has in mind there are presumably the ones in current use, the first as defined by Ed West:

> Today the term racism has come to mean almost any recognition of race...and of difference (or average differences) between groups. [*The Diversity Illusion*, Kindle location 925, quoted in "Why Isn't Racism Cool?", page 187 of this book.]

The phrase "anti-black racism" therefore means any verbal attention to negative group characteristics of blacks.

Suppose for example I say the following thing:

> Among European whites, the portion that is dumb, feckless, anti-social, and inclined to violence—call them the DFASIVs—is 10-15 percent. This is small enough that the rest can "carry" the DFASIVs, given a modest collective investment in social welfare, law enforcement, and feelgood makework.
>
> Among blacks, the DFASIV portion is much larger, 40-50 percent. The good news there is that most blacks—50-60 percent—can function perfectly well as useful, law-abiding citizens of a stable nation. The bad news is that the DFASIV portion is too big for the majority to "carry." That's why all-black polities are failures.

I guess I just committed an act of "anti-black racism," even though my negativity is aimed at only a minority of blacks (along with a minority of whites). I guess my utterance needs to be "stigmatized."

But what if the thing I just said is true, as I believe to be the case? If there actually *are* average differences between inbred human groups of different deep ancestry, then what has been stigmatized by that "campaign" VerBruggen applauds are true facts about the world.

And of course there *are* such differences. It would be biologically astounding if there weren't. Those differences are the origin of species. Thus a truth has been stigmatized and a lie permitted to prevail; and Robert VerBruggen is fine with that.

There you see the poisonous, suffocating effects of all that volcano ash. Noticing things is basic to intelligent thought. If you school yourself *not* to notice things, you become stupid.

Worse yet: If you school yourself to *pretend* not to notice things, while some lower region of your brain none the less *does* notice them, *and acts on its noticing*, then you are not merely stupid, you are a stupid hypocrite.

For a look at one aspect of the stupid hypocrisy into which the Western world has sunk, I commend to your attention the brilliant historical survey of residential segregation at *Those Who Can See*, posted a few days ago ["Whence Housing Segregation?" *thosewhocansee.blogspot.com*, December 11, 2013].

These are the depths we have sunk to, even the intelligent among us. Moral preening and wishful thinking are celebrated; true and obvious facts are stigmatized. Out of petty fears we enstupidate ourselves; for social applause and careerist opportunities, we become liars and hypocrites; and Robert VerBruggen is fine with it all.

"Seest thou a man wise in his own conceit? There is more hope of a fool than of him."

* * *

This article can be read online at http://www.vdare.com/articles/ john-derbyshire-on-race-whipped-conservatives-and-the-stigma-of-racism

What Does South Africa Tell Us About the Prospects for a Successful Multiracial State?

December 12, 2013

Nelson Mandela will be buried on Sunday December 15. South Africa will, at least until then, have the world's attention. What, if anything, does the history of that country have to tell us about the prospects for a successful multiracial state?

The official, Inner Party-approved dogma is upbeat.

> *The blacks of South Africa were cruelly oppressed by a white minority for many decades. The whites put in place a system of formalized segregation called "Apartheid," and kept the pleasant neighborhoods and good jobs for themselves.*
>
> *Blacks were forced out of areas they had occupied for generations and forced to scrape a living in barren Bantu- stans, or as servants of the whites. Those who resisted were shot down or jailed.*
>
> *Among those jailed was Nelson Mandela. The moral force of the blacks—under his guidance, and inspired by the U.S. Civil Rights struggle—together with boycotts by Western na- tions, at last wore down the will of the white minority.*
>
> *Mandela was released, and magnanimously negotiated a settlement with the whites. Full-franchise democracy was es- tablished and South Africa became the Rainbow Nation, a model for multiracial harmony, a triumph of Diversity!*

This official story is not a *totally* mendacious account of what happened, although it leaves much out. The key factor in resigning whites to a full franchise in the 1990s, for example, was not moral force so much as sheer *numbers*.

The 1911 census in the newly-founded British dominion of South Africa showed whites as 22 percent in a population of 6 million. By 1980, although their actual numbers had more than tripled, they had

167

dwindled to 16 percent in a population of 28 million, with a birthrate half that of blacks. The demographic writing was on the wall. (Whites are now nine percent in a population of 53 million, just twice the proportion of whites in 1970s Rhodesia, and of course still falling.)

The white South Africans of the late 1980s had grasped the thing we keep telling you at *VDARE.com*: *Demography is destiny.*

The feeling among whites at the time was that, absent some power-sharing accommodation with the blacks, they would be alone in a friendless world, fated to ultimate destruction.

They had, however, no illusions that their lives would be *improved* by admitting blacks into government.

> Afrikaners ceded control despite their negative expectations of black rule. "More than eighty percent believed that the physical safety of whites would be threatened. Less than ten percent believed that life would continue as before." [*Into the Cannibal's Pot* by Ilana Mercer, p. 223. Mercer is quoting Hermann Giliomee's *The Afrikaners.*]

White South Africans will tell you, too, that F.W. de Klerk, who became President in 1989 and negotiated the transition to a full franchise, was less than frank with the white electorate about his intentions, and mixed his multiracial progressivism with good doses of crony capitalism.

The key factor throughout South African history, though, has been what Cold Warriors know as the Correlation of Forces between blacks and whites. (There are other recognized races, at about one-eighth of the population, but black-white has been the dynamic that matters.)

When I was growing up in 1950s England, the oldest of the Old Soldiers were those who had fought in the Boer War of 1899-1902. Key events of that war were still part of the nation's collective memory: Black Week, Spion Kop, and of course the Relief of Mafeking.

The last of those three almost established a new verb in the language: "maffick—to celebrate with extravagant public demonstrations." The second is still remembered by supporters of Liverpool Football (i.e. soccer) Club: The stands at the south side of their stadium are to this day called Spion Kop in honor of the many men of the local regiment who died in the battle.

An elderly relative of mine, although not a Boer War veteran, would, at the slightest provocation, sing *"Goodbye, Dolly Gray,"* a song English people associated with the Boer War, though it was written for a different one.

There are plenty of printed and online descriptions of the war. James Morris gave a good impressionistic brief account in Chapter 4 of *Farewell the Trumpets*.

Here's the interesting thing: In these accounts of the Boer War, the blacks are hardly mentioned. Morris restricts himself (later herself) to:

> The Boers thought the British were resorting to genocide, and reproached them for betraying the white man's code by arming African scouts and sentries.

Not, please note, fighting soldiers.

Yet to judge from that 1911 census (there was no earlier one), blacks must already have been a majority in South Africa. It seems extraordinary that they played even less part in this white-on-white war than American blacks had in the Civil War forty years earlier.

Multiracial South Africa continued in this style through most of the 20th century as demography worked its slow magic. Whites paid as little attention to blacks as they possibly could.

Almost any mid-20th-century English person had a relative or acquaintance who lived, or had lived, in South Africa. (In my case, a first cousin.) They never talked about the blacks; nor, so far as one could tell, thought about them.

But eventually they had to. The black population simply grew faster than the white, in part due to immigration from adjacent countries, but mostly due to higher black birthrates, evolution's answer to Africa's heavy disease load.

The 1994 transition to a full franchise did not, as the liberal narrative claims, sweep away an unnatural system of separation and hostility to replace it with a more harmonious arrangement.

The separation was natural, based on universally-understood differences between the races—what Thomas Jefferson called "the real distinctions which nature has made," and what a later American statesman described as "a fact with which we have to deal."

Hostility was certainly there, but to the degree that whites thought about blacks at all, the main axis of attitudes stretched from paternalism to contempt. In the spirit of our own Cold Civil War, the real struggle was between idealistic white reformers (both Afrikaner and Anglo) and conservative white nationalists, *verligte* and *verkrampte*.

In everything but numbers, blacks were still *hors de combat*; but it is numbers that count at last.

As to having replaced the Apartheid State with a more harmonious arrangement: Well, the new South Africa is harmonious at *some* levels. What has actually replaced apartheid is an alliance of black gangster-politics and nonblack crony capitalism.

"Nonblack" there includes plenty of whites; but statistically the main beneficiaries have been Asians (a category which, in South Africa, is about three-quarters Indian, the rest mostly Chinese).

White proles are being stomped into the dirt, without even the softening consolations of elite paternalism. ["In South Africa, Whites Are Becoming Squatters," Finbarr O'Reilly, *Sunday Times* (Sri Lanka), March 28, 2010.]

Since all African politics is a struggle for tribal supremacy, white and Asian elites will eventually suffer the same fate, though with more options for relocation to new domiciles.

At the time of the 1994 deal the joke going around was:

Q: What's the difference between Zimbabwe and South Africa?

A: About five years.

This can be filed under the heading "true but premature," along with submarines, wrist phones, and the feelies.

There are several lessons to be taken from the South African experience. The main one is that white people *in numbers* have no place in Africa.

The qualifier is important: numbers are of the essence. The one percent or so of the population of Ghana that is white lives under no disabilities. As we all know, the first black family to move into the street gets the welcome wagon; the fifth or sixth gets FOR SALE signs. Numbers, numbers, numbers.

Individuals of any race can of course have amiable, indeed loving, relationships with individuals of another, but the amiability doesn't scale up. A racially homogenous society *may be inharmonious*; a society containing great blocs of different races *must* be.

Another lesson: the near-infinite capacity of people who are comfortably situated, like the white South Africans of the middle 20th century, to ignore reality. We ask ourselves: How could they not have foreseen what would come?

How, for that matter, did the 19th-century Boers and Brits, taking in the blacks of the region as cheap labor, and glossing over their commercial interest with paternalism, how did *they* not foresee the endgame?

The answer: the human capacity for wishful thinking, and our fundamental indifference to reality when it conflicts with out emotional needs or social pressures.

It is not sadism or masochism that makes us urge that the denial be brought to an end. Rather, it is a love of the reality principle, and recognition that only those truths that are admitted to the conscious mind are available for use in making sense of the world. [Garrett Hardin in *Science*, April 29, 1960.]

Of course, we can ask the same question about the GOP immigration enthusiasts. As *VDARE.com* Editor Peter Brimelow says, adapting the famous line from the old movie *Love Story*: being an immigration enthusiast means never having to say you're sorry.

* * *

This article can be read online at http://www.vdare.com/articles/ john-derbyshire-what-does-south-africa-tell-us-about-the-prospects- for-a-successful-multira

ARTICLES FROM
OTHER SOURCES

The Church of Somewhere

The American Spectator, March 2013

> When I mention religion, I mean the Christian religion; and not only the Christian religion, but the Protestant religion; and not only the Protestant religion, but the Church of England.

Thus Rev. Thwackum, the schoolmaster in *Tom Jones*. That was the 1730s, or about halfway through Roger Scruton's *Our Church*. The Rev. Thwackum is drawn satirically, but his smugness was well justified.

The religious passions of the previous century had subsided or been pushed off to inconsequential border territories in Ireland and the North American colonies. The Church of England had been incorporated into England's unwritten constitution. Her—the gender of that pronoun is explained by Scruton—bishops sat in Parliament. Her clergy, typically younger sons of aristocrats or landed gentry, were comfortably knitted in to the English class system. ("The Church or the Army" was the rule for those drawing short straws in the primogeniture lottery.)

The Church's core documents, the *King James Bible* and the *Book of Common Prayer*, were known at least in part to all educated Englishmen and had lent innumerable phrases to the common language. She coexisted peacefully with numerous Nonconformist sects and with remnant patches of Roman Catholicism. (That "Roman" prefix is necessary in this context: Reciting the Nicene Creed in their Eucharist service, Anglicans declare their belief in "one holy catholic and apostolic Church.")

Roger Scruton's book sufficiently covers the previous 200 years of the Church's history to Rev. Thwackum, and the following 280. *Our Church* is not really a history, though. Scruton keeps to a chronological sequence, but takes off on long diversions into theology, literature, hymnology, architecture, and entirely personal reflections. The book is, as Scruton says of the Church herself, "a creative muddle." Possibly some readers will dislike it on that account. For myself, I found it charming, very English.

The Church of England is easy to mock. The English themselves have never taken her very seriously, as that *Tom Jones* quote illustrates. The silly Vicar has been a stock character in English comedy and satire through Jane Austen and Trollope to P.G. Wodehouse, Benny Hill, and *Beyond the Fringe*. ("Life is rather like opening a tin of sardines: We're all of us looking for the key....") Not just silly either, but also sexually eccentric: choirboy jokes were a staple of playground humor in my own English schooldays.

Not all the mockery is well-founded. Roman Catholics jeer that the Church only exists because Henry VIII wanted a divorce. There is much more to be said than that. Henry's father had become King after decades of strife over who should succeed to the throne. Henry wanted to ensure a clear succession, for the peace of the nation, but his wife was barren. Scruton: "The refusal of the Pope to grant an annulment of Henry's first marriage was experienced by the King as a threat to his sovereignty." Henry was driven by rational statecraft, not—or not only—by sexual boredom.

Henry's break with the Papacy was, in any case, only the last act in a centuries-long record of restlessness against Roman authority among England's political elites. The English barons, pushing back after King John's groveling to Innocent III in 1213, made John sign the Magna Carta, in which the Church is referred to as *Ecclesia Anglicana*. A half-century before that there had occurred the colorful dispute between Henry II and Thomas à Becket, his Archbishop of Canterbury, centering on clerical immunity to the King's laws. (Having mentioned Becket, I want to thank Scruton for including the "à," which is nowadays usually dropped for reasons of footling pedantry.)

Henry's reforms did not go unchallenged. Among the common people of England there was still much devotion to the Roman religion, which they perceived in terms of relics, images, pilgrimages, fasts, and the doctrine of Purgatory. Eamon Duffy's *The Stripping of the Altars* describes all this in superb detail. It also, however, supports Scruton's point that "the parish priest, rather than the wealthy bishop" was seen as the true representative of the church. "Heaven is high, the Emperor far away," murmured the Chinese of old; 16th-century Englishmen seem to have felt the same about the Pope. Given the great piety of the medieval English, noted by many foreign visitors, the surprising thing is how *little* resistance Henry met. This was, remember, a regime with no standing army or police.

A key point of difference at the intellectual level was the doctrine of transubstantiation, which asserts that the Communion bread and wine actually become the body and blood of Christ. Anglican authorities were still thundering against this in Queen Anne's time (early 18th century). Scruton makes much of the dispute, arguing that:

> The revulsion that the doctrine aroused among the Elizabethan divines derived not from any rejection of sacraments but, on the contrary, from a desire to retain them—to establish a sacramental church that honestly explained itself to its members. This, in a nutshell, was the Anglican mission, and it began with Wyclif [an Oxford theologian, late 14th century], long before the Reformation had turned the order of Christendom upside down.

I am not sure why transubstantiation is less "honest" or harder to explain than its Anglican competitor, the "real presence" doctrine. As with those centuries of aristocratic restlessness, though, it is useful to be reminded that revolutions, including religious revolutions, are usually culminations of a long process, not thunderbolts from blue sky.

And when Scruton returns to his point about a sacramental church, as he does several times, he clarifies it with each returning. Thus eighty pages later we read of Scruton in the organ loft of the 15th-century English country church whose instrument (it "has one manual, three stops, and no pedals") he plays. He is musing on the institution for which he is "pumping out" hymns.

The Anglican communion is a form of sacramental religion...in which anathemas and excommunications long ago
ceased to have a point. And I rejoice that the Church to which
I belong offers an antidote to every kind of utopian thinking.
The Church of England is the Church of *somewhere*. It does
not invoke some paradisal nowhere; nor does it summon the
apocalyptic destruction of everywhere in the manner of the
seventeenth-century Puritans.

That is all very well; but does the *somewhere* that the Church of
England is the Church of, still exist? It is poignant to read Scruton,
early in his book—he is writing about the Norman and Plantagenet
kings—say this: "Our common law is inimical to laws made outside
the kingdom." Not any more it isn't, pal. England is currently bracing
itself for a flood of immigrants from Romania and Bulgaria, who
from January 1st 2014, under EU rules, cannot be denied entry, common law be damned.

The Church herself has been losing market share for decades. Entire large districts of English cities and towns are under occupation by
foreign immigrants who give not a fig for the Church, nor indeed for
Christianity. News stories about the installation of the new
Archbishop of Canterbury are decorated with gloomy asides about
dwindling church membership.

Part of the problem, Scruton notes, has been the Empire, which
diffused the Church over vast territories whose English inhabitants
later melted away, taking their Englishness with them; or in the case
of the North American colonies, rebelled...but American Episcopa-
lianism was birthed in Scotland, not England—an offshoot of an offshoot. The Church of Somewhere became the Church of Everywhere,
and therefore of course of Nowhere. As Scruton writes glumly:

Its most important controversies today—those over women
priests and homosexuality—are being fought out between
American liberals and African conservatives, with the old

English establishment looking on in mild astonishment at the fuss.

Our Church is full of good things. Scruton writes fluently, with many memorable touches. I especially liked his recollection of his teenage self at Communion, listening to the organist's improvised sequences: "It was as though the Holy Ghost himself were present, humming quietly to himself in an English accent." He has provocative insights, too, as when he writes of "the pagan heart of the Roman Catholic liturgy." He is only occasionally tedious, mostly when writing about theology, a subject in which I, along with most Anglicans (admittedly lapsed, in my case) have zero interest.

I liked this book. However, I was raised, like Scruton, in mid-20th century England, in a culture now as comprehensively extinct as that of the Moabites. Whether *Our Church* will find favor with, or even be comprehensible to, readers of different nativity, I would not venture to speculate.

* * *

This article can be read online at http://johnderbyshire.com/ Reviews/Religion/ourchurch.html

Mankind's Collective Personalities

Takimag, March 28, 2013

Here is an old Soviet-era joke, from the subgenre in which dimwitted peasant Khruschev plays Costello to smart seminarian Stalin's Abbott.

> Stalin and Khruschev are touring the East European satellites in Stalin's personal locomotive.
>
> They are sitting in the carriage chugging along when Khruschev leans over to Stalin and says: "Comrade Yosif Vissarionovich, help me please. I never know which one of these countries is which. Where are we now?"
>
> Stalin: "What time have you got?"
>
> Khruschev, looking at his watch: "Ten AM."
>
> Stalin: "Well then, according to the schedule this must be Czechoslovakia."
>
> Time passes. Again they are back in the carriage chugging along. Again Khruschev asks Stalin: "Where are we now?"
>
> Stalin: "What time have you got?"
>
> Khruschev, looking at his watch: "Four PM."
>
> Stalin: "Then this is Hungary."
>
> More time passes. Again Khruschev leans over to Stalin: "I'm sorry to be a nuisance, Comrade, but I've lost track again. Which country are we in now?"
>
> Stalin: "What time have you got?"
>
> Khruschev pulls back his sleeve to check the time. "My watch! It's gone!"
>
> Stalin: "Ah, then this must be Romania."

This joke is a slur on the noble Romanian people, whose hospitality I once briefly enjoyed. My wife also reminds me that her first dentist in the USA was Romanian, and a very fine dentist he was and apparently still is. The stereotype of Romanians as a nation of thieves is, ethnic Romanians are not shy to tell you, the fault of the Gypsies, who are especially numerous in that neck of the woods.

Here I must insert the usual disclaimer for the benefit of readers too feeble-minded to grasp sophisticated mathematical concepts such as "average" and "variation." I am sure—I have *no doubt whatsoever*—that there are many worthy and talented persons of the Gypsy ethnicity.

Gypsies in the generality, however, are bad news, working as little as they can while stealing as much as they can. Romanian Gypsies seem to embody the negative side of Gypsyhood in a particularly concentrated form. In Britain, to which they have had some limited access since Romania joined the European Union in 2007, they have specialized in stealing entire houses while the homeowners were on vacation.

("Anti-racist" hysteria has reached totalitarian levels over there, so the fact of the thieves being Gypsies is rarely mentioned. If you talk to British people, however, you will learn that, as the Brits say, "even the dogs in the street know it.")

At the beginning of next year, just nine months from now, that limited access becomes unlimited. Romanian Gypsies will then be just as British as the British, or at least as British Gypsies.

Except that they won't. I lived for 35 years in Britain and don't recall any news stories about Britons—no, not even British Gypsies—stealing the houses of vacationing fellow citizens. The "squatting" phenomenon has been around for a while, but it targets abandoned or long-unoccupied buildings.

I am speaking here of human group characteristics at the ethnic or national level. Although a deeply unfashionable topic nowadays, peculiarities of national character used to supply much of our humor, from Shakespeare's comic Welshmen to late-20th-century Polish jokes. *National Lampoon* did a fine compendium of the underlying stereotypes at about the last moment when it was possible to do so without being hauled off to the Ministry of Love for interrogation.

The concept of national character may be making a comeback, at least in Europe. One recurring theme in commentary on the troubles of the euro this past five years has been the difficulty of yoking the continent's north and south in a single banking and fiscal system. This, it has been argued, made no more sense than the idea of Silvio Berlusconi being a conceivable Prime Minister of Denmark. A *northern* fiscal union might have had a chance, people say, with the currency of course named the neuro.

Veteran British commentator Max Hastings was working this theme just the other day, writing about the Cyprus crisis:

> It always appeared absurd for the Germans, who—like the British—obey rules, pay taxes and tell the truth in financial documents, to form a financial union with the southern Europeans, who do none of those things, and are never likely to.

It may just be that big nations or unions are not a very good idea, except for purposes of self-assertion. Professor Bauer, in his fine book about the Chinese soul, passes the following remark:

> Because of the unification of the empire [in 221 BC] and its division into provinces, the sense of intimacy due to the smallness of a single state gave place overnight to the feeling that one was living in a gigantic dominion governed by a distant capital.

The subsequent history of the Chinese Empire leaves one wondering whether developments might have been happier if East Asia, like post-Roman Europe, had remained a collection of competing small feudal states.

Prof. Bauer's words might return an echo from the Britons of to-day, contemplating next January's influx of Romanian and Bulgarian Gypsies, or from the Cypriots of today gathered forlorn outside their shuttered banks, perhaps even from the Americans of today....

But hold on there. I just used the phrase "the Chinese soul." Do nations *have* souls, as different from one another as the individual human sort? Some distinguished people have thought so: Alexander Solzhenitsyn, for example:

> Nations are the wealth of mankind, its collective personalities;
> the very least of them wears its own special colors and bears
> within itself a special facet of divine intention.

Solzhenitsyn was not as wise as the leaders of the West today, who would have told him with weary patience that persons every-where are perfectly fungible, while national borders are absurd relics of parochial nativism and misguided economic protection.

How fortunate we are to have such wise leaders!

* * *

This article can be read online at http://takimag.com/article/ mankinds_collective_personalities_john_derbyshire

My Fair Lady T.

The American Spectator, April 9, 2013

Following the betrayal and defenestration of Margaret Thatcher by her colleagues in November 1990, the *Daily Telegraph* offered for sale a commemorative coffee mug adorned with a picture of the lady. I immediately placed an order, and that commemorative mug has held pride of place in our family glassware cabinet ever since.

Having learned as much, you will not be surprised to know that I mourn the passing of Lady Thatcher (as she later became). Obliged for the first time in many years to take out and examine my feelings about her, however, I find they are considerably mixed, like one's feelings towards a parent. Perhaps it is a testimony to Lady Thatcher's stature that she should have penetrated so deep into a temperament like mine, which is to say one fundamentally skeptical and not much interested in politics.

Mrs. Thatcher came to power in May 1979 just as I had concluded my *wanderjahre* and returned to Britain. Four of those *jahre* had been spent in the U.S.A., the rest in the Far East, mainly Hong Kong. By the standards of the Britain in which I had grown up, the U.S.A. was, even in the 1970s—even after two years of the Jimmy Carter presidency—an arena of unbridled capitalism. Hong Kong was more striking still. In the matter of economic freedom, it made the U.S.A. look sluggish. I had, in short, been getting an education in late-Cold War politics and economics.

I had in fact recently returned from a three-month stay in Hong Kong when the 1979 election took place. My passport stamps tell me that I had left London on January 24. It was freezing cold weather, and there was some sort of strike by the airport employees preventing the runways from being de-iced so that we could take off. We sat in the plane grumbling for an hour or two while things were sorted out. When we finally took off all the passengers applauded and cheered; not so much because we were on our way at last (I remember thinking) as from happiness at having escaped from a nation far down the dark slope of decline.

And there I was, back in the wretched place in May, in the living-room of some left-liberal friends, watching the election returns. My friends were despondent, but I found the result quite cheering. Mrs. Thatcher seemed forthright and vigorous. Patriotic, too: she had earned obloquy from the ethnomasochist Left some months before by warning of the British national character being "swamped" by mass Third World immigration. Most encouraging of all, she seemed to understand the things about economic freedom and state power that I had just recently learned during my wanderings.

The lady exceeded my expectations on all points. The heroes of Greek epic poetry all enjoyed an *aristeia*, a moment of supreme glory. Mrs. Thatcher had at least two such in her first six years as prime minister: the Falklands War of 1982, and the coal miners' strike of 1984-5. She handled both very masterfully, fortifying my belief that here at last, after decades of sycophants and cretins, was a British leader willing to defend her country and in possession of sensible views on economics. I loved her for that, and went on loving her for it.

National leadership, however, merely surfs on the mighty waves of historical circumstance. The great issue of our time in the Western world is the relentlessly increasing economic irrelevance of the left-hand side of the Bell Curve. Mrs. Thatcher's defeat of the frankly communist National Union of Mineworkers was a triumph for economic sense, but left mining towns and villages without work. Most of them remain in that condition today. As the grandchild of two coal miners from just such places, I know what has been lost.

As the horny-handed sons of toil faded away from economic relevance, Gucci-loafered young securities traders with yellow suspenders came into their own. Britain's economy shifted from digging stuff out of the ground and making and growing things to negotiating prices in a secondary market of ever more complex types of IOU. We patriotic conservatives consoled ourselves at the time by saying that at least it was better that employment should shift thus, from public-sector to private-sector employment (coal was a nationalized industry), than from private to public, as had occurred during the immediate postwar trend. Probably it was: but the shift took place at a level above the individual. Middle-aged coal miners did not get jobs on trading desks; nor, in most cases, any jobs at all. Meanwhile, public-sector employment crept upwards anyway, as it has everywhere in the West.

Thatcher's changes were necessary, but they weren't pretty. Necessary changes are rarely pretty. Politicians, however, must pick their fights and do what they can, in hopes that future generations will somehow sort out the new problems that always, inevitably, arise as old ones are solved. Things become their opposites; the chess game never ends.

Perhaps historians of the future will regard Mrs. Thatcher and her domestic enemies as Sellar and Yeatman taught generations of English schoolchildren to regard the parties in their nation's Civil War: the King's men as Wrong but Wromantic, Cromwell's parliamentarians as Right but Repulsive. I shall leave that to their judgment. I am of my time, as she was. To me, Margaret Thatcher was never repulsive, and never can be. I loved the woman, and shall revere her memory. May she rest in peace at last.

* * *

This article can be read online at http://spectator.org/print/55822

Why Isn't Racism Cool?

Takimag, April 18, 2013

We all had a lot of fun at the American Renaissance bash the other weekend. A disproportionate amount of the fun was provided by vlogger Paul Ramsey, whom I recommend for consideration when your next corporate function, birthday party, or bar mitzvah comes around.

At one point Paul mocked the little knot of anti-racist protestors camped outside the hotel. How, he asked, could this fairly be called "protest"? What did they think they were doing—sticking it to the Man? "Yo, guys: You ARE the Man!"

True enough. Time was, protest meant brave dissenters standing in proud defiance against the massed forces of Establishment power. Nowadays those massed forces believe exactly what the protesters outside our hotel believe, and they propagate it with unflagging zeal through the institutions they control: the media, business, labor, the big political parties, all branches of all federal, state, and municipal government (including the military), and all universities, colleges, schools, kindergartens, and playgroups.

The local media made the point, leaving no doubt that their sympathies were with the protestors, and ours should be likewise if we know what's good for us. The news announcers put on their most solemn *it's-painful-to-report-this-but-duty-demands* faces and quoted the Southern Poverty Law Center scam (twice!) as if it were some kind of impeccable authority, like the International Standards Organization, on metrics of "hate."

Paul's remark got me wondering, though. What's wrong with kids today? Don't they want to vex their parents? *Épater la bourgeoisie?* Kick against the pricks? Be *transgressive?*

Mildred: "Hey Johnny, what are you rebelling against?"

Johnny: "Whadda you got?"

187

Part of the fun of being young used to be the feeling that you were struggling for world mastery against a cohort of closed-minded old farts with a mentality hopelessly stuck in the past. (What Orwell called "pedants, clergymen and golfers.") Well, if it's that old-fart cohort you're looking for, check out your local Ivy League university or cable TV studio. Those places are stuffed to the rafters with them. 1963 *is* in the past, isn't it?

And these protesting youngsters believe *every single thing* the old farts believe! Their transgressions reach no further than their awful beards. The white American middle classes of today may be the most conformist population that ever lived, banking and turning in unison, old and young together, like a school of fish.

Even if these young protestors wanted to be transgressive, they wouldn't know how. Let's face it: Being transgressive isn't what it used to be. Every time I encounter it nowadays, it turns out to be dismally lame.

As an opera fan, I wondered for a while whether I should explore the transgressive delights of *Regietheater* ("director's theater"). Then I read Heather Mac Donald's survey and decided this was something I could skip without any esthetic loss:

> An American tenor working in Germany remembers another
> Fledermaus with a large pink vagina in the center of the stage
> into which the singers dived.

Zzzz. That director wasn't even *trying*. You want transgressive? I got transgressive.

- A production of Shakespeare's *Othello* in which the Moor, to his squealing masochistic pleasure, gets chained to a post and thrashed with a bullwhip by Desdemona.

- A play about feminist icon Virginia Woolf in which she dumps her drab husband, lesbian lover, and intellectual friends to go keep house for an alpha male philistine who kicks her when she's late putting his dinner on the table.

- A remake of *The Birdcage* is which it turns out that the acceptably gay Robin Williams character has been kidnapping little boys and buggering them in the club's basement.

To any youngsters seeking to get *political* transgressivity on the move again, here's a suggestion: Try racism. What could be more guaranteed to make mom swoon and dad go purple with rage?

No, no, not burning crosses on people's lawns. The word "racism" long since overflowed that little pond and inundated the surrounding lowlands. I'm talking about racism as defined in Ed West's excellent new book *The Diversity Illusion: What We Got Wrong About Immigration & How to Set It Right* that I just finished reading. Location 925 in the Kindle edition:

Today the term racism has come to mean almost any recognition of race...and of difference (or average differences) between groups.

It sure has. The last time I got called a racist (Yes! It happens!) was when I overheard someone say that the decline of Detroit was caused by liberalism. "No it wasn't," I said, "It was caused by blacks." Perfectly true, but apparently racist. *Pretend not to notice!*

Since racism as defined is transgressive, why isn't it cool? A number of answers come to mind.

- Racism can't possibly be cool because it is the most evil and depraved system of thought ever to be countenanced by sentient beings in the entire 13.82-billion-year history of the cosmos. Except that....

- Racism *is* considered cool when it's directed against white people. I bet Tim Wise ("Old white people have pretty much always been the bad guys, the keepers of the hegemonic and reactionary flame") gets invited to all the coolest parties. I bet the coolest kids on campus are the ones running Dr. Shakti Butler's ethnomasochist boot camp. ("The term [i.e. 'racist'] applies to all white people.") When Jamie Foxx boasted on *Saturday Night Live* that he got to kill all the white people in his new movie, the super-cool audience of young urban sophisticates burst into applause. The coolest Chief Executive to ever grace our republic is the one who sat in the pews for twenty years listening to the Rev. Jeremiah Wright babbling about how "white folks' greed runs a world in need."

I suspect, though, that as with most questions about human nature, the correct answer to this one can be found in biology:

Anti-racism is a mating display. It says: "Look at me! I have such earning power I can live where I like! I don't have to worry about feral underclass blacks or Salvadoran gangbangers! I can strike a pose of lofty indifference to matters of race! Drop your knickers right now!"

* * *

This article can be read online at http://takimag.com/article/why_isnt_racism_cool_john_derbyshire

The Incredible Talking Weiner

Takimag, May 9, 2013

I keep getting surprised by my own naïveté.

The case here is that of Anthony D. Weiner, who until two years ago was the US Representative from a Jewish/white-ethnic/black district of Brooklyn.

Rep. Weiner became *ex*-Rep. Weiner after Tweeting suggestive pictures of himself to female e-acquaintances and then lying about the matter. He resigned his seat, sub-editors at the New York tabloids showered so many puns and double entendres on the city that the Sanitation Department had to clear them from the streets with snow plows, and those of us who'd never seen eye-to-eye with Weiner (sorry, it's contagious) assumed we had heard the last of him—that his premature withdrawal (sorry, sorry) from public life would be permanent.

Weiner's appeal had always been lost on me, though I only knew the man from having occasionally seen him on TV. His policy positions were conventionally Jewish-left-liberal, except that he delivered them in a particularly grating way. His specialty was whipping himself up into a bogus fury decorated with bellowing mock indignation, a thin-lipped exophthalmic glare, and jabbing finger motions that could have punched through drywall. On the rare occasions a politician is justified in simulating anger, I prefer a calmer style drawn soft-voiced from a well of stillness.

And Weiner had never had any working life outside politics, a thing that always raises my suspicions of a candidate's character. If you have no other way to support yourself than by chasing votes, who knows *what* you won't say or do to stay in the arena? Weiner had never shoveled concrete for a living, or stocked warehouse shelves, or sold haberdashery over a counter, or taught a roomful of fidgeting kids, or proofed newspaper copy, or programmed computers. Having done all those things, and being inclined to self-righteous smugness about my breadwinning versatility, I looked down on the guy as a loser.

Woe to the smug! The loftiness of man shall be bowed down, and the haughtiness of men shall be made low! Earlier this year, as reported by Radio Derb, we heard that Weiner has thrust himself into (*really* sorry) the New York City mayoral race.

Given the manner of Weiner's leaving Congress, he didn't seem very electable. As the *New York Post* opined, Weiner's road to the mayoralty would surely be "long and hard." Possibly so; but at the end of April Weiner was holding his own (look, *you* try writing with a straight face about this guy) in the polls.

That wasn't what brought my naïveté home to me, though. I'd been supposing that Weiner, being out of politics, had no income; and that having no income, he was being supported by his wife, a high-level flunky in the court of Hillary Clinton. I'd been quietly enjoying the thought of Tantrum Tony sitting listless at home, wondering whether he should sign up at trade school for a course in bricklaying while waiting for Mrs. Weiner to bring home the family paycheck.

The full extent of my cluelessness was revealed to me last week by a story in *The New York Times*. "Weiner Makes Lucrative Name in Consulting," said the headline.

> It did not take Mr. Weiner long to embark on a new career after he left Congress on June 16, 2011. On July 7, he quietly incorporated a new firm, Woolf Weiner Associates, named for his great-grandfather, an Austrian immigrant to the Lower East Side.

Consulting? What does this guy know about business?

> Executives at [his client companies] described Mr. Weiner as a quick and nimble student of their businesses with an innate sense of how to navigate the rhythms and personalities of government.

Does this pay well?

> He and his wife...disclosed last week that they had a com-
> bined income of $496,000 in 2012, most of it from Mr.
> Weiner's work.

Good grief! That sure beats bricklaying. What accounted for my naïveté, though? What had I forgotten?

Probably this: that in a rich, too-big, over-governed nation, Acts
of Congress with 867 or 906 pages imposing costs and regulations on
businesses need professional legislators to decipher them for those
businesses.

Also this: that an ex-congressman married to a senior aide to the
US Secretary of State (who is also wife to an ex-president) is removed
forever from the humdrum sphere of making a living.

If you are well seasoned in politics—Weiner has clocked up 26
years—you step off that stage into a gilded world where people stuff
money into your pockets as you walk by. Weiner's boss-in-law, Mrs.
Clinton, is worth somewhere between $13-26 million. People pay her
$200,000 for a speaking appearance.

And that's small potatoes. Bill Clinton has somewhere north of
$80 million. Al Gore made $100 million just in January, though that
was a good month. Tony Blair just got paid $600,000 for two half-
hour speeches in the Philippines.

These people, please note, all belong to the Party of the Little Guy
in their respective nations: Democrat and Labour. Is the other side
coining it, too? You bet: Dick Cheney gets $75,000 a speech, "plus
first class travel for an entourage of three." But the other side is *supposed* to act like that.

I guess we shouldn't complain. There's a market and they're fill-
ing it. No doubt the National Multi Housing Council got their
$200,000 worth from Mrs. Clinton when she addressed them on April
24. She's so *wise!* Likewise with Tony Blair's speech ("The leader as
nation builder in a time of globalization") to that telecom firm in Ma-

nila. Similarly with Anthony Weiner's advice to Parabel, a firm that "harvests an algae-like crop used for food and fuel."

But were we governed any worse back when ex-presidents returned to their law practices (Coolidge) or fell back on their army pensions (Truman), while disgraced congressmen sank into middle-class obscurity?

* * *

This article can be read online at http://takimag.com/article/ the_incredible_talking_weiner_john_derbyshire

A Requiem for Science

Takimag, June 6, 2013

As a science geek from way back—Andrade and Huxley were favorite childhood companions—I try to keep tabs on that side of things. This can be disheartening. To quote from that intergalactic bestseller *We Are Doomed*:

> Scientific objectivity is a freakish, unnatural, and unpopular mode of thought, restricted to small cliques whom the generality of citizens regard with dislike and mistrust. Just as religious thinking emerges naturally and effortlessly from the everyday workings of the human brain, so scientific thinking has to struggle against the grain of our mental natures. There is a modest literature on this topic: Lewis Wolpert's *The Unnatural Nature of Science* (2000) and Alan Cromer's *Uncommon Sense: The Heretical Nature of Science* (1995) are the books known to me, though I'm sure there are more. There is fiction, too: in Walter M. Miller, Jr.'s 1960 sci-fi bestseller *A Canticle for Leibowitz*, the scientists are hunted down and killed...then later declared saints by the Catholic Church.

In a society such as the modern West, where intelligence is declining, where fertility trends are dysgenic, where cognitive elites enforce assent to feel-good ideological claptrap and the mass of citizenry is absorbed in frivolities, science hovers always on the edge of extinction. Saint Leibowitz was martyred following a nuclear Armageddon; on present evidence the Armageddon won't be necessary. We'll be barbecuing scientists for the fun of it when reality TV and smartphones begin to pall.

Even science writers seem keen to help at piling up the faggots. John Horgan, for example, who once wrote a book titled *The End of Science*, is now doing what he can to hasten that end: On the *Scientific American* blog the other day he called for a ban on research into

195

race differences in IQ. (For a take on this by the irascible but indispensable Greg Cochran, see http://westhunt.wordpress.com/2013/05/23/the-end-of-science)

Under these sorry circumstances I feel obliged to do what I can to help keep the guttering flame of dispassionate empirical enquiry alight for at least a while longer. In that spirit I recommend to you a forthcoming book titled *The Newton Awards* by Michael Hart and Claire Parkinson, now available for preorder from the publisher.

The original idea of the authors was to expand the concept of Nobel Prizes to all areas of science, technology, and math, and to award once prize per year from 1600 to 2000 AD for achievement in those fields. This couldn't be made to work exactly as planned. For the first 275 years of the period there weren't enough advances for one prize a year; for 1976-2000 there isn't yet enough perspective for good judgment. So only for 1876-1975 is there one Newton Award per year; elsewhere the awards are for 5- or 10-year periods.

The authors end up with 140 Newton Awards for the 400-year span, to 172 named awardees. Some awards go to more than one person (e.g., the Wright brothers); some persons get more than one award (e.g., Edison for the phonograph, light bulb, and distributed electricity).

The selections seem to me to be pretty good, though as a gun enthusiast I thought there should have been a mention for small-arms technology—the Minié ball, perhaps, or breech loading. (Military inventions aren't ignored: Nuclear weapons and ballistic missiles get awards.)

Political Correctness is eschewed completely, which probably accounts for the book being put out by a small publishing house. Every one of the awardees was a white European raised in Europe or one of the British-settler nations (Canada, the USA, Australia, New Zealand). Just four nations have more than ten awards each: the USA, Britain, Germany, and France.

This agrees with Peter Watson's apologetic remarks in *The Modern Mind* (2000) that:

Whatever list you care to make of twentieth-century innovations, be it plastic, antibiotics and the atom or stream-of-consciousness novels, vers libre or abstract expressionism, it is almost entirely Western.

Worse still, practically all the inventing and discovering has been done by men. Only three gals show up in Hart and Parkinson's lists, and all are joint awardees with a man: Irène Joliot-Curie (with husband Frédéric) for artificial radioactivity, Gertrude Elion (with George Hitchings) for the anti-leukemia drug 6-MP, and Jocelyn Bell (with Antony Hewish) for the discovery of pulsars.

That darn stereotype threat! Don't be looking for reviews of *The Newton Awards* in any major outlets. Being literary editor of some niche magazine isn't as much fun as working for the Heritage Foundation, but it's just as vulnerable to the Thought Police.

Reading through these achievements, a number of things come to mind. For example: What part is played by luck in these greatest discoveries and inventions? Practically none, is the overall impression. Some breakthroughs were achieved when the scientist was looking for something else or for nothing in particular; but the confirmation, elaboration, and explanation of what had been found was still creative intellectual work of the first order.

The discovery of cosmic background radiation by Penzias and Wilson in 1965, for example, was certainly fortuitous: They weren't looking for it, only trying to calibrate an antenna. Their diligence in isolating the unexpected phenomenon, though, and their collegiality in bringing in astrophysicists to provide theory, got them a well-deserved Nobel Prize.

Similarly with Antonie van Leeuwenhoek, who discovered microorganisms in 1674. The authors:

As Leeuwenhoek had not been deliberately searching for microorganisms, some books suggest that he was merely lucky. Our view is quite different. His discovery was a result of his carefully constructing scientific instruments of unparalleled quality, and then spending a great deal of time making observations with them. The combination of skill and hard work is the very opposite of luck.

Science and creative technology have, across the modern period, been the great glories of Western civilization. As that civilization yields up its lands to non-European peoples and ideologies of magic and unreason, pause to take a backward glance at the astonishing things we once accomplished: Order a copy of *The Newton Awards*.

* * *

This article can be read online at http://takimag.com/article/ a_requiem_for_science_john_derbyshire

Post-Zimmerman Fallout

Takimag, July 18, 2013

Well, thank goodness that's over. Some themes from the political and social commentary are still hanging in the air, though, like wisps of smoke after a brushfire. I'll note a few before they disperse on the breeze.

Zimmerman Is Not Racist!

The creepiest, most sinister theme has been the stories about the FBI investigation of George Zimmerman last year. From "FBI Records: Agents Found No Evidence That Zimmerman Was Racist," Frances Robles & Scott Hiaason, *McClatchy*, July 12, 2012:

> Federal agents interviewed Zimmerman's neighbors and co-workers, but none said Zimmerman had expressed racial animus at any time prior to the Feb. 26 shooting of Martin.... Several co-workers said they had never seen Zimmerman display any prejudice or racial bias.

Apparently this is a thing the feds try to determine when contemplating a civil-rights case.

I can't help wondering: What if that had been *me* they were investigating? Suppose *I* had gotten into some altercation with a black person that had ended with me killing the other party in self-defense?

I am a racist on the current definition—although, as I keep protesting, a harmless and tolerant one. Having uncovered this fact—it wouldn't take them very long—would the FBI then feel justified in launching a federal civil-rights suit against me, regardless of the finding of any local investigation into the self-defense claim?

Surely there's not much doubt that they would; otherwise, why did they put all that effort into determining whether or not *Zimmerman* was a racist?

Now, the concept of justifiable homicide is at least as old as Anglo-Saxon jurisprudence itself. The *McClatchy* report seems to imply that justifiable homicide can be prosecuted as a civil-rights violation *if* the deceased is black but the survivor nonblack, and further *if* the survivor is known to hold certain opinions, rather than certain other opinions, on social or scientific topics.

If that is the case, then our jurisprudence has been corrupted beyond redemption.

The Audacity of Richard Cohen

Washington Post columnist Richard Cohen raised shrieks from the left and some muffled applause from the right with what everyone tells me was an exceptionally audacious and hard-hitting column. Was it, though?

"I don't like what George Zimmerman did," Cohen starts off. Why not? What Zimmerman did was defend himself against a violent criminal (taking assault and battery to be violent crimes, which I believe is the common understanding) who had attacked him. What about that don't you like, Mr. Cohen?

In the next paragraph: "What Zimmerman did was wrong." Why was it wrong? The police initially, and the court system eventually, determined that Zimmerman performed an act of justifiable homicide. That might be regrettable, but it's not *wrong* in any system of values known to me.

Ah, but then we get the audacious stuff, the stuff that made the lefties swoon and some of the righties applaud (though very, very diffidently). "Where is the politician who will own up to the painful complexity of the problem and acknowledge the widespread fear of crime committed by young black males?" asks Cohen boldly.

Well, here is that politician, a solid northeastern liberal. Here *was* that politician, I should say: Unfortunately he died earlier this year, at age 88. ["Edward I. Koch, a Mayor as Brash, Shrewd and Colorful as the City He Led, Dies at 88," Robert McFadden, *New York Times*,

February 1, 2013.] He made the acknowledgment Mr. Cohen is pining for *twenty years ago*. (Jared Taylor passed a comment on it at the time in some magazine or other.)

Cohen has found his stride, though, and he presses forward fearlessly, decapitating graven images and disemboweling sacred cows as he goes:

> The problems of the black underclass are hardly new. They are surely the product of slavery, the subsequent Jim Crow era and the tenacious persistence of racism....

"Surely"! So the different statistical profiles of blacks as compared with other races on traits of behavior, intelligence, and personality are "surely" explained by slavery, Jim Crow, and racism? Good grief! How can Cohen get away with saying that in a major newspaper? No wonder people are shrieking!

> For want of a better word, the problem is cultural, and it will be solved when the culture, somehow, is changed.

The evidence out of the human-science labs is that the better word is "biological." Try putting *that* in your syndicated column, Mr. Cohen.

In the meantime, the least we can do is talk honestly about the problem.

Ha ha ha ha ha!

A Poet Speaks

Famous poet Maya Angelou had things to say about the affair, things like this:

> What is really injured, bruised, if you will, is the psyche of our national population.

I'd pass comment on this if I could understand her meaning, but I have never been able to do that. Frankly, I think Ms. Angelou is an affirmative-action bag of wind.

Come Back, Rudy

Perhaps the most dismal spectacle in current US politics is the New York City mayoral race, voting for which is this November.

You'd think that a big, bossy city such as New York, stuffed up to the subway vents with oversized egos, would produce an exciting mayoral contest. In the past it has, but this year's race is a snoozer. I've had more excitement at the all-night Laundromat. The mayoral candidates are more numerous than when I looked them over a year ago, but there's been no improvement in quality.

Veteran reporter Bob McManus agrees. "What a sad, shallow bunch," he says in the *New York Post*. He's referring mainly to their comments on the Zimmerman verdict, which are almost uniformly stupid. Samples: "A shocking insult," said far-left diesel Christine Quinn. She's polling second behind far-left exhibitionist drama queen Anthony Weiner, who called the verdict "deeply unsatisfying."

McManus singles out Republican John Catsimatidis as an exception, praising the guy's remark: "When you have safe streets, tragedies like this don't happen."

I don't know about that. It looks epistemically very thin to me, like saying: "When it's not raining, the streets are dry." By the standards of the current mayoral field, though, it's positively Socratic.

Can't we draft Giuliani back?

* * *

This article can be read online at http://takimag.com/article/ post_zimmerman_fallout_john_derbyshire

He Had a Dream

Takimag, August 29, 2013

This week marks the fiftieth anniversary of Martin Luther King's "I Have a Dream" speech. I have no recollection of the 1963 event myself, but I have good excuses for not remembering: (A) This was not my country at the time; and (B) I was in the Styrian Alps.

Well, this *is* my country now, and I'm bound to respect the national totems, of which King's speech is certainly one, so don't be looking for any ruthless deconstruction of the thing from me. I am merely going to compare King's time with ours.

First, that was an America supremely confident in our ability to do anything. We had come out of the 1940s bursting with pride and vigor into a world where our competitor nations lie in ruins. Everything was possible! The USA was buzzing with energy, creativity, and *wealth.* Heck, we could even go to the moon!

Thus Martin Luther King:

…we refuse to believe that the bank of justice is bankrupt. We refuse to believe that there are insufficient funds in the great vaults of opportunity of this nation.

Most of us would think it in bad taste to talk like that in a time of seventeen trillion dollars of national debt and a looming entitlements overhang. And we sure won't be going back to the moon anytime soon. These are more sober times, with lower hopes and expectations.

Second, we are a lot less religious now than we were then. King's biblical diction, those quotes from Amos and Isaiah, would be lost on hearers nowadays. Blacks are still more religious than nonblacks, but even black leaders—even Sharpton and Jackson—don't talk like King anymore, not outside church anyway. Barack Obama sure doesn't.

(American friends of the older generation tell me that even at the time, educated blacks made fun of King's rhetorical style. Those blacks were yuppie agnostics, scornful of Bible-quoting Southern

rubes. A lot of them, including some senior figures in King's entourage—notably Jack O'Dell—were members of the Communist Party.)

Third, King made it sound a lot easier than it turned out to be. He
was reaching for low-hanging fruit: segregation laws, voting tests,
police brutality. King's listeners believed that once those obstacles
were swept away, blacks would rise to equality with whites.

Well, the obstacles *were* swept away, and then some. Not only
was discrimination against blacks outlawed; discrimination *in their
favor* was legislated across major areas of American life—in college
admissions and in government hiring, promotion, and contracting.

Yet the equality didn't happen. Huge differentials in crime, academic achievement, and wealth accumulation remained. In some
cases, they *increased*.

The best-documented crime is homicide, where there is a corpse
to be accounted for: Blacks commit homicide at seven to eight times
the nonblack rate, according to statistics published by Eric Holder's
Department of Justice. In academics, every measure—from NAEP to
LSAT (Figure 14)—shows black mean scores a full standard deviation below the nonblack means. For median household wealth, the
Census Bureau reports whites at *twenty times* the black level, and this
gap seems to be widening.

Since the statistics can't be denied—they are too plentiful and
consistent—we deny that there has been any change in the causative
factors. Black-opportunity-wise, we pretend it's still 1963. The obstacles preventing black success have become vaporous and abstract yet
somehow have kept the same height and weight. We have retreated
into magical thinking, away from the large and the loud, indeed away
from anything visible or audible, into a shadow world of poisonous
miasmas and unseen forces, of *djinns* and *dybbuks*.

In 1963 we had No Blacks Need Apply; now we have "institutional racism." Then we had schools segregated by law; now we have
"stereotype threat." Then we had separate drinking fountains; now we
have "white privilege." Then a black voter was kept from the polls by

being asked to spell the word "paradimethylaminobenzaldehyde";
now he has to—*gasp!*—show a driver's license. Then we had Sheriff
Rainey; now we have "hate."

Our intellectual elites, who would scoff at astrology or witchcraft,
all subscribe to this essentially magical style of thinking. Thus that
very elite magazine *The Economist*, August 24th issue:

> Discrimination has not vanished: the recent decision in New
> York to outlaw stop-and-frisk searches reflects the fact that in
> many places the police remain far more likely to suspect and
> harass innocent blacks. Voter-ID laws, while no doubt rooted
> in partisan rather than explicitly racial motives, still place a far
> heavier burden on minority voters than on white ones.

Never mind that New York City's impeccably liberal Mayor Michael Bloomberg has argued, with supporting numbers, that *whites* are
overrepresented in stop-and-frisks. Never mind that nobody can explain how it is a "far heavier burden" on a black than on a nonblack to
produce ID at a polling station.

This retreat into magic horrifies me more than any particular
atrocity. It is an appeal from civilization to barbarism, a rejection of
all the hard-won understandings of these past 400 years. Most horrify-
ing, most shameful of all, our highest seats of learning are approving
this nonsense, this gibberish of savages.

Ah, but if we were to drop the magic we would find ourselves
face to naked face with nature, which ordains all sorts of terrible
things. She ordains earthquakes, plagues, mass extinctions, and the
divergence of separated breeding populations. We'd prefer that these
horrors didn't apply to our precious selves; but alas, nature couldn't
care less what we prefer. Best cling to the magic, then.

Martin Luther King, in that pious America of two generations ago,
could rest his hopes on a God-ordained equality in potential of all
human populations, needing only a field cleared of gross obstacles to
come fully into view.

We look at those stubborn statistics, thinking of the decades of upheaval and the trillions of dollars spent, and wonder.

* * *

This article can be read online at http://takimag.com/article/ he_had_a_dream_john_derbyshire

The Stupid Wars

Takimag, November 21, 2013

I was in England for Remembrance Sunday this year. The wreath-laying ceremony at the Cenotaph was very moving. I had forgotten how much emotion the British invest in this and how high a proportion is imaginatively keyed to WWI. Remembrance Sunday is defined to be the Sunday closest to Armistice Day, November 11, when the guns fell silent on the Western Front in 1918.

It is a cliché—true, of course, like most clichés—that every nation has a special place in its collective heart for its bloodiest war. For Americans that would be the Civil War. Being a half-century further in the past than WWI, the Civil War doesn't engage American emotions as strongly as WWI does the Brits of today. Possibly things were different in 1961. I wasn't here in the USA; I don't know.

The notion of WWI that I grew up with in 1950s England was of the Stupid War. British social antagonisms at that time revolved around class, so that the stupidity was attributed to the ruling classes, with General Haig the emblematic figure. The poor brave Tommies were "lions led by donkeys," Haig being the Donkey-in-Chief. The whole war was pointless and unnecessarily prolonged, and Upper-Class Twits were to blame.

By the 50th anniversary of the war in 1964, this had become received wisdom among Britain's educated classes. It found definitive expression in the stage musical, later a movie, *Oh! What a Lovely War*. (Long Island's Adelphi University is doing a revival next month.)

Professional historians have since gone through their customary cycles of revisionism and re-revisionism. Haig has plenty of defenders, as does the principle that small, weak countries in vulnerable locations, like Belgium, should be able to rely for survival on treaty arrangements with bigger neighbors.

Treaties aside, Britain's decision to go to war can be seen in the long context of that nation's ancient fear of a single power controlling continental Europe: Spain in the 16th century, France in the 18th, Russia in the Cold War. Any power that attained European supremacy, the British reasonably believed, would soon turn on *them*.

Even the German and Austrian decisions that got the war rolling were based on reasonable, or not wildly *un*reasonable, premises.

For all that, though, and with due allowance for the well-known optometric precision of hindsight, WWI was by any rational assessment of costs and benefits a monumentally stupid war; though the stupidity was general, not restricted to any section of society. The original decisions may have been reasonable, but once thousands had died the Sunk Cost Fallacy took hold, dooming millions more.

Four great civilized empires (Russia, Germany, Austria, and Turkey) were shattered and a fifth (Britain) was holed below the waterline. Non-Europeans lost what respect they'd had for the world-bestriding white race and turned away from the notion of the West as a mentor.

Kipling's fevered warning that "the Hun is at the gate" and the boast inscribed on the Victory Medal that this was a "war for civilization" were absurd. The Germany of 1914 was, by general agreement, the most civilized, most advanced nation in Europe, as Bertrand Russell—whose first published book was on German politics—testified:

> The Kaiser's Germany, although war propaganda on our side represented it as atrocious, was in fact only swashbuckling and a little absurd. I had lived in the Kaiser's Germany…. There was more freedom in the Kaiser's Germany than there is now in any country outside Britain and Scandinavia.

(That was written in an essay forty years after the event. Russell's memories of the outbreak of war, recorded in his *Autobiography*, are also worth noting. Sample: "I had supposed that intellectuals frequently loved truth, but I found here again that not ten per cent of them prefer truth to popularity....")

On a cost-benefit analysis, indeed, many wars are extremely stupid. I believe this is true of the American Civil War. As many observers have noted, slavery was abolished in all the other European colonies and ex-colonies without the mass slaughter of 1861-65. Was the sacrifice of more than 600,000 young Americans really necessary? Would it really have been a greater evil to let the South go?

Similarly with the Vietnam War, the stupidity of which was eventually apparent to enough Americans to undermine the entire enterprise. Indochina ended up communist anyway, and the sky did not fall. Well, it fell on the Indochinese, but not on the USA, as advertisements for the war had threatened. National-interest-wise, the thing was futile.

You can argue that *all* wars are stupid. Jonathan Swift did so in Part IV of *Gulliver's Travels*, when Gulliver explains to the perfectly rational Houyhnhnms why Europeans go to war: "Sometimes one prince quarrels with another, for fear the other should quarrel with him. Sometimes a war is entered upon because the enemy is too *strong*, and sometimes because he is too *weak*...," etc.

Not many of us would go that far. What option but war did the Finns have in 1939 or the USA in 1941? In mass-suffrage societies wars are anyway often popular. WWI was so in Britain; Lincoln had no difficulty raising his volunteers; and the Vietnam War had majority support until 1967. Who dares defy the popular will?

Still, the components of stupidity, fallacy, and wayward emotion in driving the greatest wars can hardly be denied. That's worth bearing in mind when you hear geostrategic blowhards talk about "rational actors."

If there *were* any such in 1914, there are fewer today. China, which just forty years ago was in the grip of a quasi-religious mad despotism, has nuclear weapons. So does North Korea, the plaything of a teenage voluptuary. So does Pakistan, an anarchic slum populated by superstitious peasants and ruled by thieves. Who next—the Congo? Even the civilized nations of the West are rapidly being en-stupidated by mass immigration.

More Stupid Wars in our future? Stupid *nuclear* wars? Bet on it.

* * *

This article can be read online at http://takimag.com/article/ the_stupid_wars_john_derbyshire

The City of Brass

Takimag, December 12, 2013

Little more than a hundred years ago the modern British welfare state was born in David Lloyd George's 1909 finance bill, the "people's budget." Hearing of the bill's provisions—old-age pensions! unemployment benefits! land taxes! (in those innocent times it was thought prudent to pay for social programs with taxation)—Rudyard Kipling was furious. He vented his fury in a poem, "The City of Brass," 32 couplets of anapestic pentameter thundering with internal rhymes.

The gist of the thing was that Kipling's countrymen, "smitten with madness" by their commercial and imperial success, had given themselves over to fantasies of social perfection, egged on by demagogues—"prophets and priests of minute understanding":

> *They rose to suppose themselves kings*
> *over all things created—*
> *To decree a new earth at a birth*
> *without labour or sorrow*
> *To declare: "We prepare it today*
> *and inherit tomorrow."*

Ants were to be punished, grasshoppers rewarded:

> *They said: "Who is eaten by sloth?*
> *Whose unthrift has destroyed him?*
> *He shall levy a tribute from all*
> *because none have employed him."*

Criminals were to be set above the law:

> *So the robber did judgment again*
> *upon such as displeased him,*
> *The slayer, too, boasted his slain,*
> *and the judges released him.*

211

The people, led by demagogues, "awakened unrest for a jest" among the subject peoples of the Empire and "jeered at the blood of their brethren betrayed by their orders."

Worse yet, they mocked the bourgeois virtues:

> *They nosed out and digged up and*
> *dragged forth and exposed to derision*
> *All doctrine of purpose and worth*
> *and restraint and prevision.*

It was all a bit splenetic. Kipling worked the general theme much better—more soberly, more reflectively—ten years later in "The Gods of the Copybook Headings." If you are feeling splenetic rather than reflective, though, the earlier poem suits your mood better. And yes, that's how I'm feeling, looking across the Atlantic to the land Kipling loved and to which I still have, I confess, some emotional connection.

Here, for example, is a story that got my spleen overheating. Sergeant Alexander Blackman of the Royal Marines has been given a life sentence at court-martial for shooting dead a wounded Taliban captive in Afghanistan. He was told he would serve at least ten years, which is around normal for the number of years that *civilian* murderers serve in Britain. (The average is 14 years, but this average is pushed up by very long terms for the worst kinds of murders—of children, police, etc.)

The shooting occurred in Helmland Province, in a zone of intense combat—"the most dangerous square mile in Afghanistan," in which captured British soldiers have been skinned alive. During Sgt. Blackman's tour, 23 men from his brigade were killed. That's around one in 200. I can't find a number for the maimed, blinded, crippled, and emasculated, but I'm told that under modern medical conditions in the field, the ratio of wounded to killed is about six to one.

The incident was filmed by a camera mounted on the helmet of one of Sgt. Blackman's colleagues. The purpose of such cameras escapes me. It has been famously said that we lose respect for laws and sausages when we have seen them being made. War can fairly be added to the list, I think. Probably the intention here is to ensure that British infantrymen carry out their traditional tasks—defined by Bernard Montgomery as "to find the enemy and kill him"—without violating anyone's human rights.

Sgt. Blackman, who has a spotless 15 years with the Marines through several combat assignments, will serve his sentence in a civilian prison. This is significant, as Britain's prisons are hotbeds of Muslim extremism. Sgt. Blackman will be a prize target for glory-seeking jihadists, as will his family following the fool judge's decision to release their names.

The cruel absurdity of this prosecution becomes clearer if you play out the counterfactual. Suppose Sgt. Blackman, instead of offing the Taliban (with a quip from Shakespeare: "Shuffle off this mortal coil, you cunt") had administered first aid. The Taliban, though very badly hurt by cannon fire from a helicopter gunship, might then have recovered.

And then…what? Captured Taliban members are handed over to the Afghan authorities for trial and sentencing. Given that a 2012 NATO report on the fighting "abounds with accounts of cooperation between the insurgents and local government officials or security forces"—and noting in passing, with regard to Sgt. Blackman's sentence, that 15 years for planting IEDs is "an extremely long sentence by Afghan standards"—captured Taliban fighters probably anticipate their handover with good cheer.

The war itself is, of course, perfectly pointless. Sgt. Blackman's 23 comrades died to no purpose, as he is surely intelligent enough to know, while the repulsive rodent who sent them there takes a break from harvesting six-figure speaking fees to pose with his sad face at the memorial service for that other maker of IEDs, Nelson Mandela. You want spleen? I got spleen.

That's the war in Afghanistan I'm talking about there. The *other* war, the one our elites really care about—the war in which Sgt.

Blackman's prosecution has been a minor skirmish—is going swell. That would be the war against heterosexual white males, especially those of a military inclination.

Had Sgt. Blackman been a black man, or homosexual, or a woman, this incident would have been swept under the rug. But then, he would not likely have been in 3 Commando. Britain's special forces, like ours, are overwhelmingly white, as blacks mostly gravitate to the three-hots-and-a-cot service jobs. Homosexuals are made very seriously unwelcome. Women can't meet the physical standards.

How will it all end, this modern insanity of "diversity," "human rights," and futile missionary wars for the propagation of Cultural Marxism? Probably as Kipling tells us:

> *For the hate they had taught through the State*
> *brought the State no defender,*
> *And it passed from the roll of the Nations*
> *in headlong surrender!*

* * *

This article can be read online at http://takimag.com/article/ the_city_of_brass_john_derbyshire

RADIO DERB

Radio Derb

May 4, 2013

Intro

And Radio Derb is on the air! Yes, this is your transcendentally genial host John Derbyshire, broadcasting from our state-of-the-art sound studio here on Taki Theodoracopulos's private island in the sunny Aegean.

Spring has arrived here in the Mediterranean, and the goddess Persephone has come up from the Underworld to bless us with fertility. No doubt soon the rich soil of our island will be bringing forth its fruits.

Speaking of which, I see Nikki Nicolaides coming up from the village on his donkey with our lunchtime order of goatburgers.... Brandy, take care of Nikki, would you, my dear?... Thank you....

Immigration Bill Boosters Showing Flop Sweat

When "comprehensive immigration reform" came up this time around and we heard that the Senate Gang of Eight were working on a bill, my heart sank.

We had been here before, of course. Three weeks from today, in fact, on May 25th, you can celebrate the 7th anniversary of the U.S. Senate passing the Kennedy-McCain Comprehensive Immigration Reform Act of 2006. Thanks largely to widespread opposition from the American public, that Act died in committee and was buried in a pauper's grave when Congress wound up after the 2006 mid-term elections.

When the globalist elites want something, though, they'll keep pushing till they get it. Our foremost political philosopher, the great P.J. O'Rourke, has observed that the people who get what they want in politics are the ones who keep the meeting going longest. Normal people with lives, hobbies, and kids, get bored and drift off back home at eight or nine o'clock. The ones who are still in the hall at eleven o'clock are the ones who get their resolution voted through.

My local school board does something similar. They make us vote on a budget. We vote it down. They move three or four words around in the budget proposal and make us vote again. Eventually everyone but the activists gets bored with voting and stays home, so the activists get their way at last, or most of it. European Union referendums work the same way. Make Joe Public keep voting till he's sick of the whole business; then Annie Activist, Billy Bureaucrat and Charlie Capitalist get what they want.

I thought Comprehensive Immigration Reform was some similar scheme: just keep bringing it up until voters get bored and it slips through by default.

I am now beginning to get the happy feeling that my pessimism was misplaced. Opposition this time seems even stronger than it was in 2006. It's cruel to say so, but the Boston bombing has helped a lot, highlighting the follies and stupidities of current refugee resettlement policy.

The Bill pushers are starting to look like a vaudeville act that went on the road confidently expecting applause and success, only to be met with half-empty houses and catcalls from the balcony.

Steve Sailer has resurrected the old vaudeville expression "flop sweat" for the unpleasant physiological reaction a stage performer goes into when he realizes his act is bombing. Steve says there is a definite aroma of flop sweat rising from the appearances of the Bill pushers. Marco Rubio has conceded that the Bill won't pass the House of Representatives without some tightening-up in the enforcement aspects. Barack Obama, meeting with Latino race—or if you prefer, "raza"—lobby leaders at the White House this week, told them they're not going to get everything they want.

The problem here is that even the bill as currently written doesn't give the Latinos what they want. They're *already* grumbling. Quote from "Obama Prods Liberals to Give-and-Take on Senate Immigration Bill," Kevin Nakamura, *Washington Post*, May 1, 2013:

> Angelica Salas, executive director of the Coalition for Humane Immigrant Rights of Los Angeles, was among a group this week that criticized what members called the excessive hurdles in the bill for undocumented immigrants to gain legal status.

Just to remind you, those "excessive hurdles" include inhuman atrocities like a $500 fee.

So tightening up the Bill to improve its chances in the House is just going to rile up the Latinos even more. Yet even Rubio and Obama concede it's un-passable as it stands. So this thing could die in committee like the last one did. Most encouraging.

As against all this optimism, you have to wonder how much the congresscritters really care about Latinos. The real point of this Bill is to drive down American private-sector wages by flooding the labor market. The real driving force behind the Bill is the great scads of money being shoveled into congressional pockets by the agriculture lobbies, the hotel and casino industries, the big software firms, and so on. The battle isn't over until *they* give up.

They're not going to give up easy. I see in this week's news that Facebook's Mark Zuckerberg is financing a big new open-borders lobbying effort. Marco Rubio may be dripping with flop sweat, but the fight isn't over yet, by a long way.

Comprehensively Hating Americans

For citizens arguing, in private or in public, against the immigration bill, here are a couple of pressure points you should work on.

I hit the first pressure point in conversation with a neighbor while back Stateside recently. I had mentioned the folly of importing twenty million or so new citizens when millions of existing citizens can't find work. In response my neighbor mentioned a relative of his who runs a small business requiring some manual and low-level technical work.

"He has this guy from El Salvador working for him," said my neighbor. "A great worker, conscientious and punctual. He can't get Americans willing to work like that."

"So," I said, "you're telling me Americans are no good."

This stopped him dead. My neighbor's a decent guy, patriotic and ex-military. He was lost for words. "No!" he said at last, rather indignantly, "that's not what I'm saying."

"But you told me your nephew can't find an American worker as good as this Salvadoran guy. Isn't that saying Americans are no good? How isn't it?"

My poor neighbor got all flustered and tongue-tied there. "No, I'm not saying that. Absolutely not! It's just that Americans aren't...they can't...they need training and...education."

By that point he was just babbling nonsense. I started to feel guilty, and changed the subject.

There's probably a nicer and friendlier way to work that pressure point with ordinary decent Americans like my neighbor. My social skills aren't up to much. The pressure point's there, though, and needs working.

Closely related to this widespread notion that immigrants are better workers than Americans, is the idea that immigrants are more entrepreneurial than Americans. That's a big favorite with globalist elitists like Michael Bloomberg, Mayor of New York City.

In fact rates of entrepreneurship overall are lower for immigrants than for natives; and in the biggest immigrant groups they are *way* lower. Mexican immigrants over age 25, for instance, had a self-employment rate of 7.8 percent as of March 2007, the latest numbers I can find. For Dominicans it was 5.1 percent. For Hispanic immigrants as a whole, 7.5 percent; for all immigrants, 11.3 percent. For natives: 12.6 percent. Those lackluster, non-vibrant, boring and lazy Non-Hispanic White natives: 17.2 percent.

Of course, mere facts aren't going to stir a conceited blockhead like Bloomberg. I wasn't the least bit surprised to see his name on the list of sponsors for a new lobby called The Partnership for a New American Economy. What does this partnership want? Quote: "to raise awareness of the economic benefits of sensible immigration reform."

That wouldn't be anything to do with business moguls wanting cheap labor, would it? Let's see, who else have we got on the sponsorship list? Bill Marriott, as in Marriott hotels. Bob Iger of the Walt Disney Company—amusement parks, hotels, and cruise ships. Steve Ballmer of Microsoft. Ri-i-i-ight.

More Vile Slanders Against a Great Man

This week has seen further vile conspiracies against our dear friend, President Gurbanguly Berdymukhamedov of Turkmenistan.

The President is among his many other talents a superb horseman. Last Sunday he rode in a race to showcase a breed of horse he himself has sponsored, the Akhal-Teke. This was in Ashgabat, the splendid capital of Turkmenistan.

Such was the skill and horsemanship of President Gurbanguly Berdymukhamedov, he placed first in the race, against competition from the best jockeys in Central Asia.

This was wormwood and gall to the President's enemies, who are legion. They manufactured some bogus video footage of the President being thrown from his horse after crossing the finish line. This fabricated footage has been circulated with much glee by those traitors and saboteurs who seek to denigrate the achievements of this great world leader. They have compounded their crime by putting about the story that this mishap actually occurred, but that news of it was suppressed by Turkmenistan broadcasting authorities.

At Radio Derb's subsidiary in Ashgabat—which, thanks to the generosity of President Gurbanguly Berdymukhamedov, is the main, in fact the *only* radio station broadcasting in Turkmenistan—we have been at pains to quell these evil rumors and to uncover the evil slanderers behind them. They will meet appropriate punishment, never fear.

In other news from Turkmenistan, the final auction of shares in the Karakoram pipeline, bringing natural gas from the nation's deserts to the Persian Gulf ports, was concluded in Ashgabat this week. The auction was held behind closed doors, but it is believed most of the shares went to an unknown investor based in the Aegean.

Long live President Gurbanguly Berdymukhamedov! Long live the noble republic of Turkmenistan!

[Clip: Turkmen national anthem.]

Human Affairs Aren't Math

I have a strong temperamental aversion to watertight and inflexible public policies. In last week's broadcast I argued for a ban on immigration from majority-Muslim nations. A listener emailed in to put the following case to me: A U.S. combat soldier stationed in some Muslim country falls in love with a local girl, a Muslim, and marries her. Then he's badly hurt in an IED explosion and shipped back to the States. Should his wife be allowed to join him?

My answer was: "Of course she should! What do you take me for? Why would anyone think she should *not*?"

That last question is rhetorical: I don't know why anyone would think we should exclude a Muslim in that situation. The human world is full of oddities, exceptions, and cases that don't fit any grand watertight schema. Laws need to be written with some wiggle room, though of course you can always argue about how much wiggle room is *too* much. Should that Muslim lass be allowed to sponsor her parents for settlement, or her siblings? I'd say no, but there are fair arguments on the other side. What if she's a widow with teenage Muslim kids; can she bring *them* in?… Discuss among yourselves.

A great many people *do* like their policies watertight and inflexible, though, and seek to turn public policy into a kind of Euclidean geometry, in which conclusions follow remorselessly from axioms, with no space for variations or exceptions.

Those people should always be resisted. Not that I've got anything against mathematics: I have a degree in the subject, and I've written two books about it. It's just that human affairs aren't *like* that. The watertight-and-inflexible people are committing a category error.

There is probably no area of public policy where this category error is more rampant than in the matter of abortion.

On both sides of the abortion issue there are people—*lots* of people—committing the category error, trying to reduce the human world and all its smelly muddle to geometry.

On the right-to-life side you have the argument that as soon as sperm has fused with ovum you have a unique individual, a *person*, the destruction of whom is a form of murder, or at least manslaughter. On the right-to-choose side you hear that control over one's own body is an absolute and fundamental human right, so that up to the snipping of the umbilical cord, decisions about zygotes, embryos, fetuses, and newborn babies are the mother's alone, and anyone who wishes to interfere is committing a hateful act of patriarchal oppression.

Radio Derb's position is that early abortion is so commonly desired, and so easily accomplished, there are no strong reasons to oppose it; while late abortion is offensive to common sensibilities and ought to be severely restricted; and that the legal line dividing "early" from "late" should be something we can arrive at by general consensus, as we do with things like drinking age.

Not only is that Radio Derb's position, it is also the position that all states of the Union, and most nations of the world, adopt, though there are differences in the details. In more liberal jurisdictions, that line between early and late is put at the point of viability, the point in a pregnancy where the child could survive outside the womb, most commonly set in law at 24 weeks, though there are cases of babies surviving earlier than that.

Children that *do* survive outside the womb are of course entitled to all the care we can give them, and killing them is homicide. Practically nobody disagrees with that. Certainly no civilized law code disagrees with it.

Other jurisdictions have tried to push the line back. Nine American states have banned most abortions beyond 20 weeks. Two states have recently gone further: Arkansas has banned abortion after 12 weeks and North Dakota beyond the point where fetal heartbeat is detectable, which is usually around six weeks. Pro-abortionists are challenging these statutes, though; and given the disposition and previous rulings of the U.S. Supreme Court, the challenges will likely win.

Just for a check on current stats, according to the Centers for Disease Control, 92 percent of current abortions are performed before 14 weeks, with 1.3 percent beyond 20 weeks.

Be all that as it may, nobody but right-to-life purists are much disturbed about 8-week abortions; and nobody but right-to-choose purists are *not* disturbed about 28-week abortions. Euclidean geometry doesn't work here: we are in the zone of human sensibilities—of empathy and pity, of disgust and shame, of argued compromises and arbitrary lines.

Policy and law here are driven by common feelings; and, to borrow a sentiment from David Hume, so they should be.

For example: There are now some remarkable techniques for imaging fetuses in the womb. I'll hazard a guess that as these techniques get even better, and more widely known, public opinion will push that line between early and late back to earlier, down below 20 weeks everywhere. We won't have any more knowledge than we had before; we won't have been persuaded by arguments we never heard before; it will only be that having clearer images of that fetus in the womb will change our *feelings* about it, and that will change laws and policies; and that, in my opinion, is as it should be.

That's just an orientational preamble to the next segment, on the case of Kermit Gosnell.

Dr. Gosnell's House of Horrors

Dr. Kermit Gosnell, 72 years old, is an abortionist who was practicing in Philadelphia until his license was suspended three years ago. A year after *that* he was arrested and charged with several counts of murder.

Gosnell went on trial seven weeks ago. Arguments have now been heard, and the jury is deliberating as Radio Derb goes to tape. The most serious of the charges they're deliberating are four of first-degree murder for killing living infants and one of third-degree murder for overdosing a mother with Demerol, causing her death.

The court testimony was gruesome. You need a pretty strong stomach to read much about this case. I'll just give a brief sample from the testimony of Kareema Cross, who worked at Gosnell's clinic for four years. This is from an April 18th court report on CNS News. Long quote:

"Did you ever see those babies move?" asked Prosecutor Joanne Pescatore.

"Yes, once in the toilet," said Cross.

The baby "was like swimming," she said. "Basically, trying to get out."

Adrienne Moton, an employee at the clinic, then took the baby and snipped the back of its neck while the mother was still in the room.

Cross told the jury that when Shayquana Abrams came into the clinic in July 2008 she was pregnant, "and she was big."

"That was the largest baby I ever saw," Cross said.

When the baby was born alive, Abrams was sleeping. Cross said Dr. Gosnell took the baby boy, which she described as 12 to 18 inches long, and put him inside a plastic container the size of a shoebox.

"The baby was still breathing," she said. "He didn't cut the neck right there."

The baby was too big for the plastic container, with his arms and legs hanging over the sides.

"The Doctor cut the back of the baby's neck but didn't do suction—normally Dr. Gosnell would do suction...to suck the brains out," Cross said.

"I called people over to come see it [the baby] and we took pictures," she said....

"It was supposed to go upstairs in the freezer, but it was still there the next day because the janitor complained," Cross added.

She said Dr. Gosnell told her "the baby is big enough that it could walk to the store or the bus stop."

Eventually the baby boy went in the freezer, Cross said.

Grisly stuff. They have the death penalty in Pennsylvania, though they haven't used it since 1999. If Dr. Gosnell goes to the gurney, I sure won't be shedding any tears for him; although the way death penalty cases drag through the courts nowadays, the rat will be in his nineties before he gets the needle.

This is one of those stories, though, where the sidebar issues have generated as much talk as the crime itself.

There have been two sidebar issues. One: Was this case under-reported because most reporters are liberals and liberals are big fans of abortion? Two: Was this case under-reported because Gosnell and most of his staff and patients were, as you may have divined from the names there, black, and reporters go easy on blacks?

On the first one, I have to register agnostic. If somebody wants to give me some money to do a thorough statistical study of the reportage and compare it with similar cases, after giving me a good robust definition of "similar," I'll take your money and give you a solid answer. Based on half an hour's googling, I don't see it.

For example: A Google search on the website of the Philadelphia Inquirer with key "Gosnell" returned, quote, "about 3,000 results," with dates going back at least—I confess I didn't check all 3,000—at least to 2010, before Gosnell was arrested. The New York Times covered the opening of the trial March 18, and they'd covered Gosnell's indictment back in 2011. True, they didn't front-page it; but murders of any kind are rarely front page copy.

And I see that when conservatives began complaining that there wasn't enough reportage, liberals pushed back by noting that *conservative* outlets hadn't exactly been all over the story. A Fox News reporter first showed up in the courtroom four weeks into the trial, actually the same day as an MSNBC reporter first appeared. By mid-trial the *Washington Times*, our leading conservative broadsheet newspaper, had run just one story on it that I could find, and that depended on a wire service report.

On the second, I do rather strongly suspect that if this had been a white doctor killing black babies, or a white doctor killing white babies, or even a *black* doctor killing white babies, we'd have heard more about it.

Gosnell's attorney, reaching for the race card in his closing arguments for the defense, took the opposite tack. He said that the Philadelphia district attorney's office was pursuing a, quote, "elitist, racist prosecution." Further quote: "Dr. Gosnell is not the only one doing abortions in Philadelphia, but he was an African American singled out for prosecution," end quote.

Again, though, as a cold empiricist, I'd like to see a careful comparative study. Why don't the big media firms, with all their resources, do one? Why doesn't Fox? Why doesn't the *New York Times*?

So I'll stand agnostic on both sidebars here. I can't resist noting one little detail on that second sidebar, though. It's a little snapshot of race and class in America today.

Gosnell had a white employee named Eileen O'Neill, who presented herself as a licensed doctor, even though she wasn't one. He also had a black employee, Tina Baldwin, completely untrained in medicine or nursing and originally hired as a receptionist. Both these women administered medications, helped with procedures, and wrote prescriptions.

Tina Baldwin, that's the black one, testified in court that Ms. O'Neill, that's the white one, kept her office neat, in contrast with the rest of the clinic, which was filthy and disorderly. She further testified that Gosnell steered wealthy or white patients to O'Neill's office. Quote from Tina: "Nine out of 10 times, if the patient was white...he didn't want me to [give the medications], because he wanted to meet with them himself," end quote. Tina said that Gosnell told his staff, quote, "that's the way it is," end quote.

Yep, that's the way it is.

Fat Boy Jerks Our Chain

Kenneth Bae, an American citizen of Korean ancestry, has been sentenced to 15 years hard labor in North Korea for hostile acts against the state.

Mr. Bae was arrested last fall after entering North Korea as a tourist. South Korean activists say he was trying to photograph starving North Korean children. Mr. Bae is a Christian who has done charity work on behalf of North Koreans.

What's going on here is that North Korea is looking for some respect, preferably a high-profile visitor. They've done this before in recent years, kidnapping visitors and giving them bogus sentences, then freeing them after a visit from Jimmy Carter in one case, Bill Clinton in another. Perhaps they're hoping for George W. Bush this time.

The newspapers are saying that the Norks are mad as hell over (a) the joint U.S.-South Korean military exercise held recently, and (b) the recent tightening of U.N. sanctions against them.

Maybe. The North Korean ruling classes, though, when you see them on TV, don't look as though sanctions are causing *them* much distress; and I'm sure they have our measure well enough to know there is zero chance we will attack them.

In a dictatorship like that, everything is internal. Kim Jong-un needs to keep showing his people what a big man he is. Copping a visit from a U.S. ex-president is a good way to do that. *Look*, it says to the North Korean masses, *your president's a PLAYER!* It makes the masses proud, and those it doesn't make proud it makes fearful. Who'd even *think* of going against a guy who swings that much weight in world affairs?

Mr. Bae was very foolish to go into North Korea, knowing they have done this kind of thing before. It's almost impossible to stop our citizens committing this kind of folly, though we should certainly try. Our national interest is to stay well out of these annoying situations, and patriotic citizens should try to help us do that. So my sympathy for Mr. Bae is considerably limited.

Still, we are the U.S.A., with a status to uphold among the nations of the world. We should try hard to think of something we might do to vex the Norks, really tick them off. Something undercover would be best: A mysterious explosion in some oil terminal, something of that sort.

My fantasy solution here, for future reference by U.S. administrations: Space needles. What you do is, put up a satellite loaded with long javelin-like rods of some heavy metal—space needles. You have a mechanism to kill the orbital velocity of one needle, or a group of needles, so that it or they just drop right down through the atmosphere under gravity. You could aim them with great accuracy. The kinetic energy when they reach the ground would be terrific, easily enough to destroy one of Kim's villas…or an oil terminal. No fallout, no bomb-casing fragments, easy deniability.

In my dreams the Pentagon, under highest-level secrecy, already has such a satellite in orbit. In practice, of course, I know that this administration would never be that imaginative.

Miscellany

And now, our closing miscellany of brief items.

Imprimis: It's been a while since I rode my hobby-horse about how you should GET A GOVERNMENT JOB if you know what's good for you. Well, Bryan Caplan at *econlog* has dug up some numbers from early last year that make the point yet again. And these numbers are from the CBO, the Congressional Budget Office.

1. After adjusting for education, occupation, work experience, and other observable characteristics, federal salaries are only 2 percent higher than in the private sector. *But….*

2. Federal workers' fringe benefits are 46 percent higher than in the private sector. So….

3. Total compensation (salary + benefits) is 16 percent higher for federal workers than comparable private sector workers.

The CBO also found that overcompensation is highest for the *least*-educated federal workers—36 percent higher than the private sector if you've got a high school diploma or less. So if you're an educational failure, you should *especially* GET A GOVERNMENT JOB!

Item: The story goes that when P.T. Barnum told his assistant that there's a sucker born every minute, the assistant responded: "OK, but where do all the others come from?"

That assistant's wisdom was verified last week in Epsom, New Hampshire, when 30-year-old Henry Gribbohm of that place attended a traveling carnival show. There was one of those games where you throw balls into a tub and win prizes—ultimately an Xbox Kinect. Mr. Gribbohm kept throwing those balls until he'd thrown $300 worth. Then he went home and got his life savings, $2,300, from under the mattress and played some more, till he was broke.

Never let it be said that carny barkers have no heart. When Mr. Gribbohm grumbled about having lost all his money, the barker took pity and gave him a prize. No, not the Xbox: he gave him a 6-foot stuffed banana with dreadlocks and a Rastafarian bonnet. He also gave Mr. Gribbohm $600 back, leaving him only $2,000 out of pocket...mattress, whatever.

The Xbox Kinect sells for $231 on Amazon.

Item: A couple of animal stories to round off the news. Everyone likes animal stories.

The Russians have launched a satellite into orbit containing forty-five mice, eight Mongolian gerbils, fish, snails, plant seedlings, and an unspecified number of geckos. One of the project scientists, Pavel Soldatov of the Institute of Biomedical Problems, tells us that, quote, "They go through selection stages no less stringent than the astronauts.... The animals selected must be social animals, used to living with others." End quote. They must also be ready to die with others; on return to earth the animals are euthanized for detailed study. I just hope that irritating gecko from the insurance ad is among the astro-critters.

One more animal story: The President of Botswana has been wounded by a cheetah. A government spokesman said it was a freak accident and there were, quote, "no real security implications." So I guess the secrets of Botswana's nuclear program are safe for the time being.

Signoff

There you have it, ladies and gents.

I do apologize for that little spasm of optimism there. Out of character, I know. It did bring something to mind, though. Here is the great New Zealand soprano Kiri Te Kanawa *dis*-proving the notion that opera singers are no good at singing anything that isn't opera.

More from Radio Derb next week.

Radio Derb

October 5, 2013

Intro

And Radio Derb is on the air! Yes, this is your eternally genial host John Derbyshire with news from far and wide, brought to you courtesy of *Taki's Magazine* from Taki's private island in the sunny Aegean.

If you tuned in last week you'll recall that we had to end the broadcast prematurely as a mob from the village was besieging the studio here, blaming us for Mayor Papakonstantinou's outrageous insult to the island's virgins. Well, we had a miraculous deliverance from the wrath of the mob. We were in fact saved by politics—a most unusual occurrence in my experience.

You see, just as I was herding all my employees into the safe room, villagers with iPhones got the news about the government in Athens arresting Golden Dawn leaders.

Golden Dawn, I should explain, is the nationalist party here in Greece. It's a serious party, with 18 seats in the Greek parliament and support polling around 15 percent recently. Here in the Aegean, where we see a lot of illegal immigrants coming over from Turkey and North Africa, there are many Golden Dawn voters.

So when the villagers got the news about the government arresting Golden Dawn MPs, they turned around and headed back to the village where the government party has an office, to vent their rage on that. A narrow escape for us, and not much harm done, I'm glad to say.

There are some big international issues behind the Golden Dawn arrests, so let me take a look at those before I get on to other news.

Camp of the Saints

A big part of the problem here is illegal immigration. Yes, I know it's an issue back in the States; but it's an even bigger one here in Greece. Here's a little-known fact: 90 percent of illegal immigrants in the European Union entered the continent via Greece. Ninety percent. Obviously a lot of that ninety percent keep right on going, to Britain, Germany, France. A lot don't, though; and the ones who do, are in Greece long enough to be a problem just in transit.

The illegals are pretty much all either Muslims or black Africans. The Muslims come from the Arab countries or from West Asia— Pakistan, Iran, Afghanistan. The Africans are from all over sub-Saharan Africa, but mainly from the eastern part—Somalia, Eritrea, South Sudan.

They enter mostly from Turkey; either by sea across the Aegean, like the Iraqi hero of Derek Turner's excellent novel *Sea Changes*, or else across Greece's 125-mile land border with Turkey, up in the far northeast of Greece.

It doesn't help a bit that there's bad blood between Turkey and Greece going all the way back into the days of the Ottoman Empire— you may recall Lord Byron had words to say about that. Nor does it help that Turkey is miffed at the European Union, to which Greece belongs, for not letting Turkey in. Turkey's turn towards the east and towards Islam in recent years adds another layer of unhelpfulness: the Turks have been relaxing visa rules for Muslim countries and encouraging cheap flights into Istanbul.

So Muslims and Africans have been pouring into Greece for years, tens of thousands every year just across the land border. And they are coming into a nation in dire economic straits. Unemployment in Greece is 28 percent; youth unemployment—ages 15 to 24—is *62 percent*. It's not surprising that there's resentment against the illegals. What's surprising is, that there isn't *more* resentment.

This is a huge and swelling problem for Europe, most especially for nations like Italy and Greece, those closest to the Third World regions east and south of Europe. Just take a look at the numbers. I get mine from the CIA World Factbook.

Take for example *per capita* annual GDP, which in the U.S.A. is $51,000, near enough a thousand bucks a week. In Eritrea, the source for a lot of these illegals, it's $800. That's *17 bucks* a week. In Somalia, another big source, it's $600; in Afghanistan, $1,100—almost up to 25 bucks a week. Greece, for all that it's in such dire economic straits, posts $25,000. That doesn't look so dire to a guy from Somalia.

And things will get a lot worse before they get better. Check out the age structure in these countries. In Eritrea, 41 percent of the population is younger than 15. Forty-one percent. In the U.S.A. it's twenty percent. In Somalia, another big source, *44 percent* of the people are younger than 15. In Afghanistan, 43 percent. The number for Greece is 14 percent.

So let 'em in, you might say. If you work for *The Economist* or the *Wall Street Journal*, that's what you *will* say. Plainly Europe needs more young people, while Africa and West Asia have surpluses. What could possibly go wrong?

What could go wrong is that the numbers wishing to come are so great, and their cultural connection to Europe so slight, and the failure of their home countries to develop rational government so total, the smart money would have to bet on major social disruption, cultural conflict, and political collapse.

Europe's Nationalists

Hence nationalist outfits like Golden Dawn. Most European countries have them. (I haven't checked Luxembourg or Andorra.)

In style, these nationalist parties fall on a spectrum, from sober middle-class suit'n'tie outfits like Britain's UKIP and Geert Wilders' Freedom Party in the Netherlands, through France's National Front and Austria's Freedom Party, to the somewhat more rambunctious Sweden Democrats, out to the street-fighting extremes of Jobbik in Hungary.

To the liberal media they are all "far right," if not "Neo-Nazi," but these designations don't often make much sense. The economic programs of these parties are protectionist, sometimes frankly socialist, which isn't what you'd expect on the right wing.

As for "Neo-Nazi"; well, the 1930s just don't map well onto the 2010s, and personally I think it would clarify our thinking if we could all forget about the damn Nazis. None of these parties is planning to invade Poland. There *is* anti-Semitism in some of them, especially Jobbik; but while Israel is independent, prosperous, and bristling with nuclear weapons, I'm not going to worry too much about the welfare of European Jews. In this age, the Jews can take care of themselves.

As much as I hate to give an inch to the leftist media, however, some of these parties practically beg to have the "neo-Nazi" label stuck on them. Golden Dawn is a case in point. The party emblem is a twisty-S symbol that you can't help thinking was designed to bring swastikas to mind. Nikos Mihaloliakos, the Golden Dawn party leader, is on record as a holocaust denier.

Golden Dawn is somewhat to the wilder end of that spectrum of European nationalists, in fact, with a street-fighting element among its supporters—though it has to be pointed out in that context that Greece's innumerable leftist factions are by no means averse to a spot of street fighting themselves.

Our revered proprietor, Taki Theodoracopulos, summed it up very succinctly: Golden Dawn is, he said, quote, "not house-trained."

There are a few things to bear in mind here, though. A big one is, that Greece was occupied by the Wehrmacht in World War Two. Patriotic Greeks, including Taki's father, maintained a heroic resistance, and many of them died in Gestapo torture chambers. Taki tells the story of one such patriot in his 1991 memoir *Nothing to Declare*, pages 46 and 47. So Greek nationalism and Nazi sympathies don't travel comfortably together, whatever Mr. Mihaloliakos thinks.

Another thing is, that Greek politics is rougher than the average. Forty years ago, remember, Greece was ruled by a military junta who'd seized power in a coup. When contemplating Greek politics, you need to be more in a Latin American frame of mind than a European one.

So, what happened last month was that a Golden Dawn supporter, described in some outlets as a party member, stabbed a leftist activist to death in a street brawl. The lefties took to the streets in a big way, burning cars and attacking police, and the government, a coalition of center-right and center-left, blamed Golden Dawn for the trouble. Last weekend they arrested Mr. Mihaloliakos and four other Members of Parliament and several party activists.

The goverment's tactic may have worked. This may be the beginning of the end for Golden Dawn. Polling since the arrests shows a big drop-off in public support, and after an initial spell of anger, pro-Golden Dawn demonstrations have been scattered and feeble.

Be that as it may, the government is stomping on the symptom, not addressing the problem. Greece in particular, and the European Union in general, needs to get a grip on illegal immigration into the continent. If they don't, the public feeling that put Mr. Mihaloliakos and his colleagues into parliament will find some other outlet, perhaps one even less house-trained than Golden Dawn.

Obamacare—Not Unpopular *Enough*

OK, over to the U.S.A., where the week has been dominated by two big news stories: the rollout of Obamacare and the shutdown of the federal government. Let's take them in turn.

October 1st, the first day of fiscal year 2014, was supposed to be the day that Americans signed up to these federally regulated and subsidized health care exchanges. How'd that go?

Not well. Neil Munro at the Daily Caller reports that on the first day in California, which has exceptionally high levels of poor and uninsured people, *not one person* registered at the exchanges, though half a million visited the registration website. Likewise in Kansas, according to Rep. Tim Huelskamp of that state. Kansas has 365,000 uninsured residents; not one signed up.

Connecticut did a little better: 167 applicants registered for insurance. I don't have data for other states yet, but it doesn't look very good.

Now, speaking as an old systems analyst, I know things don't always go well on a first roll-out. On the other hand, I also know that they rarely go *this* badly. This thing is in trouble.

Americans don't much like Obamacare, and never have. Its passage, without a single Republican vote in either the House or Senate, was one reason the Democrats lost the House in 2010. Americans just don't like their politics that partisan.

Americans still don't much like it, but they don't much like the idea of defunding it, either, and for the same reason. It's a paradox, but those are the numbers: 54 percent of voters in a Fox News poll want to see all or part of Obamacare repealed; yet voters are against defunding the law by 53 to 41 percent. Defunding is just too partisan.

Here's a prediction. If the registration glitches can be sorted out, the American public will come to a grumbling, complaining acceptance of Obamacare. The wonks who write the blogs tend to forget that not many ordinary citizens care about politics. They just want the crowd in Washington D.C. to get on with things, keep things running. They don't expect high standards: the expression "good enough for government work" is understood by everybody. They just don't want paralysis and breakdown.

If Obamacare doesn't go into a total technological brain freeze, or implode from too many healthy people choosing the tax penalty rather than the insurance premiums—a thing the feds can easily fix by jacking up the penalties—Americans will sigh and put up with it.

Pushing unpopular measures through the legislature just because you can, because your party controls the legislature, is bad statecraft. In fact it's dangerous: that's how the Spanish Civil War got started. Unfortunately Obamacare just wasn't *that* unpopular.

We should curse the Obama administration for what it did— arrogant and undemocratic as it was—but face the fact that it wasn't unpopular enough to lose Democrats the Senate in 2010 or the Presidency in 2012.

I hate it, but that's how it is. My guess is, we're stuck with the damn thing.

Republicans Putting Up a Fight!

That's my guess. I could be wrong, though. I was wrong last week about the government shutdown. Quote from me, quote: "Congressional Republicans do *not* want to be the guys who shut down the government. They remember the last time they tried that, with Bill Clinton in 1995. It didn't end well for them."

End quote. Well, apparently congressional Republicans *do* want to be those guys. OK, just hold on while I scrape this egg off my face…there.

It's gutsy, and you don't often get to say that about anything the congressional GOP does. The President's being gutsy too, though, in his own way, flatly refusing any revision of Obamacare, letting the GOP take it right to the cliff edge—to the upcoming debt limit negotiations, that is.

The President and his Senate backers have a lot going for them. Controlling the executive branch, they have some leeway about which parts of the federal government are shut down. They can work it to make the shutdown as ugly and painful as possible, and as much to their own advantage.

They can, and they have. Most famously, they decided the WW2 memorial in Washington should close. So we got pictures of elderly veterans who'd flown across the country to pay respects to fallen comrades, not being able to get into the park. You're supposed to think: "Those heartless Republicans, shutting down the government!" If you *don't* think that, the administration's shills in the media will prompt you to think it.

Less famously, but more revealing of the administration's mentality, employers trying to use the E-Verify system to check that a job applicant is legally resident in the U.S., found this week that E-Verify is a victim of the shutdown. E-Verify makes it harder for illegal aliens to get work. Naturally that causes the administration to hate it.

And the President can say things that give the stock market the jitters. Could Congress fail to raise the debt ceiling, putting the nation in default? someone asked him. Sure they could, said the President, and the Dow fell 140 points.

So all credit to House Republicans for battling on into these headwinds. I doubt this will end with the defunding of Obamacare, but we might yet win some concessions from this cynical, arrogant administration. If we do, I'll be glad to have been proved wrong.

Errata: Putin, Possums, and Precincts

Speaking about being proved wrong, I need to set up some kind of system for dealing with errata.

Errata are things you get wrong. Not general opinions like that last one, but points of simple fact. Radio Derb's superb staff of highly-trained professional researchers do a terrific job of assembling our news stories here, but sometimes Homer nods, or Mandy imbibes one glass of ouzo too many, and a correction is in order.

For example, in last week's broadcast I said some unkind things about Vladimir Putin, who started out in life as a KGB operative in the old Soviet Union. He has blood on his hands, I said, actual blood on his actual hands. I referred to him as a, quote, "leg-breaker."

That brought a response from a gentleman with a Hungarian name, who emailed in as follows.

He never did anything like that. The KGB, which means "Committee for State Security," was a huge organization, including border guards, political police (but not ordinary police), foreign intelligence, counter-intelligence, and a few similar areas. It even had some military units (which were so secret that even the army high command knew nothing about their whereabouts). You have to understand that secret (or political) police work was a small part of this huge organization.

This huge organization had a huge number of bureaucrats in its ranks. Putin was one of them. He was a lawyer by training, who excelled in writing reports. For the leg-breaking they needed someone else. Moreover, he never worked for the secret police, he worked for counter-intelligence for one year and then after for more than a decade for foreign intelligence, and these two directorates did virtually no leg-breaking at all. In the U.S. foreign intelligence, Putin would have been an excellent PowerPoint specialist. He would never be a good leg-breaker, because apparently he never ever did any kind of real work himself. But we can be sure he wrote excellent reports, and I'm sure if they had PowerPoint projectors, he would have made excellent PowerPoint slides.

Well, thank you, Sir—or should I say *köszönöm szépen*? I am willing to take your word for it. Indeed, as has been noted many times by many observers, much of the evil in the world is done by desk jockeys with PowerPoint presentations. Probably Kim Jong-un is watching a PowerPoint presentation even as I speak. As a friend of mine likes to say: Power corrupts, and PowerPoint corrupts absoutely.

And then, in the previous week's broadcast, I reported on the new Australian Prime Minister being unable to move into his official residence begause it was infested with possums. A possum, I explained, is a little marsupial, found only in Australia and New Zealand. That brought in a *lot* of email. Sample:

There's possums in my back yard in California. Gotch'ya.

Another sample:

We do so have marsupials in Texas. In fact, a possum frequents my back yard. He sneaks indoors to eat my dry cat food. I've eaten the little buggers at a barbecue. Grilled armadillo with a black pepper rub ain't bad neither.

Well, it's nice to hear from different parts of the country, but here's what my Merriam-Webster's says, quote:

POSSUM *noun* Any of several species (family *Phalangeridae*) of nocturnal, arboreal marsupials of Australia and New Guinea. *See also* OPOSSUM.

When I go to "opossum" I get this, quote:

Any of about 66 species (family *Didelphidae*) of New World, mostly arboreal, nocturnal marsupials.

End quote. So it seems that what you have in the states there is *o*-possums; not merely a different species, nor even a different genus, but actually a different *family*. You may *call* them "possums," leaving out the initial "o," just as you may, if you want to be disrespectful, call the President "Bama," but you are committing a solecism.

I am therefore going to claim victory in this little controversy, henceforth to be known as Possumgate.

One more: Listing off America's wealthiest counties last week, to show you how depressingly many of them belong in the Washington, D.C. metropolitan area or thereabouts, I said that Loudon County, Virginia is, quote, "right next to Arlington County."

An indignant resident of the Old Dominion emailed in to expostulate, thus: "Loudoun County is *not* contiguous to Arlington County. They are separated by Fairfax County. See attached map." And my kind listener actually attached a map.

My sniveling apologies to the residents of Northern Virginia. Let's hope that will stop Robert E. Lee's spinning in his grave....

Miscellany

And now, our closing miscellany of brief items.

Imprimis: One activity of the federal government that the administration will absolutely not shut down is nuisance lawsuits by the Department of Justice against states and municipalities for infractions against political correctnness.

Two such cases have recently been announced. In the first, Eric Holder is suing the Fire Department of Austin, Texas for racial discrimination. What's happened is, the Fire Department selects recruits using a test of firefighting knowledge and general knowledge. Blacks and Hispanics pass the test at lower rates than whites. *Ergo* someone must be discriminating.

Yeah, yeah, it's an old story. What we need here is for someone to come up with a test relevant to firefighting that blacks and Hispanics, in the generality, pass at the same or higher rates than whites. How hard can it be? There must be lots of black firefighters around the country by now, after all these lawsuits. Let *them* write the test. *They* won't discriminate, will they?

Some years ago I recall reading about a psychology professor who was convinced that written tests were all biased against black Americans. He devised a test oriented towards black culture, with questions like "In what year was Martin Luther King born?" and "Who led the great slave rebellion of 1831 in Virginia?" He gave the test to mixed groups of black and white students. Alas, the whites outscored the blacks.

Item: Eric Holder's other excellent adventure, announced on Monday, is to launch a lawsuit against the state of North Carolina to block that state's stringent new laws on early voting and voter i.d.

I can't help noticing that North Carolina is a swing state. Mitt Romney won it by 50 percent to 48 percent in 2012.

This business about voter i.d. laws being racist is obviously bogus in a country where you have to show i.d. to buy beer or get on a plane. Is this just political, to give Democrats the chance to flip swing states? Are any solid red or solid blue states being sued? I'm just wondering.

Item: A 40-year-old male and a 30-something female were walking home from a party together in the Ukrainian city of Zaporozhye on Saturday morning when they were overcome by lust. Not just ordinary lust either, but the kind of lust that wants some spice, some danger to intensify it.

The couple accordingly lay down on nearby railroad tracks and commenced an act of sexual congress.

Unfortunately they had not thought to consult a railroad timetable. While they were *in medias res*, a train came...I mean, came along. I don't know why the train didn't stop. Perhaps there wasn't time; or perhaps the driver heard the lady shouting "Don't stop! Don't stop!" and obeyed her command. I don't know. Anyway, the lady was killed and the gentleman lost both his legs...as well as, I'm guessing, his rhythm.

Now the poor fellow has to get his life back on track. [Boo, hiss.]

Item: Microaggression of the week: The British supermarket chain Tesco has an online store. One of the items in that store was an inflatable gay best friend. Yep, it's a life-size inflatable doll that...looks gay. No, I don't really get the point, either. Quote from the product description:

Ready with an inflatable bunch of roses to cheer you up after any break-up or bad day, your new g*y best friend will be at your side whenever you need a hug.

End quote. Yes, I know what you're thinking: "Is it anatomically correct?" I really, *really* don't want to know.

Anyway, here was the microaggression: That product description and all the accompanying material spelt "gay" as g-asterisk-y. That had all the homosexual spokes-poofs flapping their arms in protest. Screeched one, quote: "It's a shame that Tesco have chosen to represent gay men in such a narrow-minded way, ignoring the true diversity of the gay community. What is more disappointing is that their website censored the word 'gay', when the term is neither offensive nor risqué."

Squealed another one, quote: "Clearly, some people still subscribe to stereotypical views of gay people and these views continue to have negative consequences for gay people," end quote.

Oh, surely not. I find it hard to believe that after all these years those tired old stereotypes are still current. Boy, there must be some real Neanderthals out there.

Signoff

And that's it, ladies and gentlemen. October is upon us, and the season of mists and mellow fruitfulness...especially for those of us with an inflatable gay best friend. I hope all my Stateside listeners are busy carving pumpkins and erecting scarecrows. I'm afraid there are no pumpkins on the island here; only olives, which are *really* difficult to carve.

In keeping with the season, here to see us out is Yves Montand singing about *les feuilles mortes*, the dead leaves.

More from Radio Derb next week.

AFTERWORD

Afterword: Premature Immigration Patriots

By John Derbyshire

The poet assures us:

> *To side with Truth is noble,*
> *when we share her wretched crust,*
> *Ere her cause bring fame and profit,*
> *and 'tis prosperous to be just.*[6]

I have been sharing Truth's wretched crust with the *VDARE.com* collective since July, 2000. Her cause does not yet bring fame or profit; but on the topics we concentrate on here—issues related to the National Question—there has surely been progress.

To be sure, the Left still controls most of the commanding heights in our society: the schools and colleges, corporations, the courts, labor unions, most of the media. Public discourse on National Question issues, however, is increasingly slipping out of their grip.

Fifteen years ago a regular reader of political magazines and newspaper op-eds could go for months without seeing an article about immigration, for example. The Left never spoke of it; while among opinion journalists on the respectable Right there was a general feeling—I know there was: I was mingling with them—that the topic was out of bounds, and that to hold opinions about it marked one as eccentric and vaguely disreputable.

Nowadays journalists of all factions have the word "immigration" set up in their word processors as a single-key macro, and luminaries of the milquetoast Right give public speeches that would not have looked out of place as *VDARE.com* columns in 2000. There has definitely been progress.

---

[6] James Russell Lowell, "The Present Crisis" (1845).

That is the case with the topic of *illegal* immigration, at any rate. It is still heterodox to offer any opinion on *legal* immigration other than enthusiastic approval. Indeed, it is normal for public figures to preface negative remarks about illegal immigration with an assurance that *of course* they welcome legal immigrants—the more the better! Is not legal immigration the very essence of America, the source of our wealth and the fount of our values…, etc., etc.?

We can reasonably hope, though, that with illegal immigration now an everyday topic of political conversation, other issues related to the National Question—multiculturalism, race relations, federalism, citizenship, immigration in general—will soon be opened to honest, critical discussion.

This is already happening with race relations. The stupendous levels of black criminality are much more mentionable now than was the case 15 years ago. Respected political voices—Rudy Giuliani's, in a news story current as I am writing this—speak frankly about it, in a way they would not formerly have done.

Some of these changes in acceptability have been brought about by sheer numbers. Quite remote parts of the U.S.A. now have colonies of immigrants from the poorest, most culturally distant regions of the Third World ("Somalis Find New Home in Cheyenne," *Wyoming Tribune-Eagle*, November 25, 2014.) Mass immigration has turned three major states majority-minority: California, Texas, and New Mexico.

As *VDARE.com* contributor Steve Sailer says, the first commandment of Political Correctness is: Stop noticing things! However, as your state, city, or neighborhood fills up with foreigners practicing dramatically different folkways, it gets harder and harder not to notice.

In the older, more ethnically conservative nations of Europe, the number of noticers has reached a critical mass, sufficient for them to form plausible political parties. In France, Britain, and Scandinavia (see page 130 above), these parties are in the ascendant. There has so far been no comparable political coalescence in the U.S.A., but there is no reason to think it impossible.

The failure of social engineers over several decades to shift racial disparities in statistics on crime or academic achievement has likewise made it harder to continue not-noticing *those* things.

With each decade of failure, the ever more fanciful social-science explanations for the disparities—culture of poverty! stereotype threat!—are ever less persuasive, making innate race differences in behavior, intelligence, and personality correspondingly more thinkable.

Parallel to these social changes, and reinforcing heterodox ways of thinking about National Question issues, have been scientific advances in areas like genetics and paleoanthropology, enlarging our understanding while narrowing our expectations of how much human nature can be shaped by social programs.

When the history of these changes comes to be written, there will be no better source for the historian than the archives of *VDARE.com*. Where we have led, meeker spirits have followed, usually at intervals of several years.

Survivors of the 1930s democratic Left in Europe described themselves bitterly in later years as "premature antifascists." We at *VDARE.com* are the premature immigration patriots. When, as will surely happen, our cause one day brings fame and profit, and 'tis prosperous to be just, we promise not to be bitter.

You have already helped that cause—the cause of Truth—by purchasing this book, for which we thank you. If you want to give further support to *VDARE.com*, please consider a tax deductible donation to the VDare Foundation, using the form that follows this Afterword.

Now, could I share a piece of that crust, please?… Thanks.

To support *VDARE.com* make a
tax-deductible donation to the VDARE Foundation!

Visit www.vdare.com/contribute for information about donating
online, anonymously or by fax.

Mail check to: VDARE Foundation
                   PO Box 211
                   Litchfield, CT 06759

                   (Form provided for your convenience!)

Name: _____

Address: _____

City: _____

Zip Code: _____

Email: _____

Phone: _____

Amount: ☐ $50

           ☐ $100

           ☐ $500

           ☐ Other $ _____

CPSIA information can be obtained
at www.ICGtesting.com
Printed in the USA
BVHW091003200123
656618BV00007B/890